D1726985

Job Interview

Will These Mistakes Cost You The Job?

Contents

Introduction

It is a pretty safe bet that everybody, at some point, is going to have to face a job interview. Whether it's searching for your first job after graduation, looking for new opportunities, or heading back to work after taking some time off, you are going to have to go to an interview. The most important step in getting a job is the interview. You might get noticed with an amazing resume, but the impression you make during the interview is what will make sure that you get the job.

There is no such thing as being too prepared for an interview. This includes researching the company to rehearsing the answers you can give, to the interview where practice is extremely important. Whether you are experienced or not, interviews are one of the most nerve-racking things you will ever do, and they can prevent very qualified people from getting the job.

There are different parts of the interview process, and they are all just as important as the other. This includes the clothes you wear, the things you say, and what you do once it ends. This book is here to help answer all of the questions you may have when it comes to preparing for a job interview. Through studying the information in this book, you will gain the confidence that you need to make it through your interview process.

This book will take you through every part of the interview process; before, during, and after. It also provides you with some vital information concerning what employers want and why simple mistakes will cost you the job.

This book will walk you through the most common mistakes made when applying for a job. This could be resume mistakes or how you answer the questionnaire on the application. You want to make sure that you get the interview so you can shine.

Then we will look at mistakes made before you go into your interview. This means you have impressed them with your application, and you have received the call for an interview. Now comes the time for you to get ready for the actual interview. This will include how you dress and how you prepare for the interview.

Then we will walk through some of the common mistakes that are made during the interview. These are probably the most important things to prepare for. You will learn that talking badly about your previous employer, no matter how bad he or she was, is a huge no-no, among other things.

To wrap things up, we will look at examples of good and bad interviews so that you can start to see what you should and should not do. If you are experienced in interviews, you may start noticing things that you have been doing that has cost you the job that you wanted.

Lastly, to make sure that you are always prepared for a job interview, you will find a job interview checklist at the end of the book. This will help you make sure you have done everything possible to make the best first impression.

By following the tips and ideas found within these pages, you can improve your odds of landing your next job and impressing the interview panel. This book will help you to become a success.

What Do Employers Want?

One of the main things people want to find out before an interview is what an employer is looking for, or what they want. The natural and simple answer is: leaders who can work well as part of a team.

In 2016, the National Association of Colleges and Employers (NACE) released a survey on *Job Outlook* and over 80% of those who responded said that employers are looking for evidence of leadership skills on a person's resume. Almost all of these people are also looking for candidates who can work on a team.

Within the same survey, employers also said that a strong work ethic, problem-solving skills, and written communication skills are essential for a potential employee. Employers give more weight to verbal communication skills than they do quantitative or analytical skills.

While hiring managers do look at your academic major, GPA, and extracurricular activities, leadership roles can help you to stand out amongst the other candidates.

As Richard Branson said, *"Hiring the right people takes time, the right questions and a healthy dose of curiosity. What do you think is the most important factor when building your team? For us, it's personality."*

While in an interview, the interviewer wants to get to know you. Your resume has told them everything that they need to know about your job skills, work history, and education. You will have to answer questions based on this information, but to blow them away, you have to speak beyond what is on your resume.

Each company has its own 'approaching the interview' process. Some will ask everybody the same question while others have a more open approach, allowing the conversation to flow naturally. There are a few things, as an applicant, which you can do to make yourself stand out amongst the competition. These are the things that employers are looking to see:

Understand the Company

"Never hire someone who knows less than you do about what he's hired to do." – Malcolm Forbes

The interviewer is going to want to know that you are familiar with the company. Before you sent in your resume, you should have researched the company to find out what it is that they do, how it's structured, where it operates, and other bits of information. This information is helpful during the interview so that you can show them that you have the skills and knowledge needed for the job. They don't want to hear generic answers to their questions; instead, tailor your response to show them how you would handle their company's specific needs.

It's Yours to Lose

Since the interviewer is looking to hire somebody who has your skills, and the process of hiring people takes up their time and takes them away from their regular duties, they typically come into the interview wanting to offer you the job. What you have to make sure you don't do is provide them with a reason to change their minds.

Show Success

"If you think it's expensive to hire a professional, wait until you hire an amateur." – Red Adair

As long as you show the interviewer that you can work well with others, make sure you "toot your own horn". They want to know about your success, especially those that relate to the position you are interviewing for. To make your life easier, make sure you come prepared with a few stories about things you have achieved.

Are You Answering the Questions?

While getting ready for your interview is excellent, and you should spend some time studying the kinds of questions that might be answered when it comes to the interview, you have to listen. Listen to what they ask and answer those questions. You don't want to answer their question with a practiced answer that has nothing to do with what they asked.

Make sure that you listen to their complete questions and give them a natural response. If you allow yourself to jump ahead and start thinking about how you are going to answer while they are still talking, that is going to annoy them. Trust that you can find your own words. You want to be conversational. This is going to help you connect with them.

They Want to Like You

"Don't hire anyone you wouldn't want to run into in the hallway at three in the morning." – Tina Fey

Since they know you have the skills they need, and they want to hire you, what do you want to get from the interview? Honestly, they are looking to see if they like you and if you will fit well into their team. Once you have been hired, you are going to be a person that they see and talk to every day. It is important that they know you because they are going to be spending a lot of time with you.

If you come off cliché with your answers, you aren't going to impress them. If you try to make your answers too perfect, they aren't going to learn about who you are—this will probably also annoy them. Make sure you are friendly and personable. Be a conversationalist instead of stating rehearsed answers. Build rapport with them.

Body Language

Are you sitting up straight? Being relaxed is a good thing, but slouching is not. You should be sitting up straight, looking professional, but also natural. Also, take note of any fidgets or crazy body movements you may make. Things like clicking a pen, picking at your nails, or tapping your finger can distract your interviewer from what you are saying.

Make sure you also add a warm smile as you speak, but keep it natural. Having a wide crazy green is not going to help you get the job unless you are applying to be a smiley face. Also, just because you are nervous, don't think that is negative. Interviewers expect you to be a bit nervous. Try your best to practice a little beforehand, be yourself during, and make sure you make eye contact. Most likely, this is going to help you relax enough to be yourself, and that is all that you want.

Your Looks are Important

The way you look when you come into the interview does impact whether or not you get the job. If you are dressed too casual, you will likely come off unprofessional or not serious enough about the job. If the hiring manager or the company has specific issues with odd facial hair, visible tattoos, or multiple piercings, these could also cost you the position. If you appear flustered, sweaty, and nervous, they may think that you aren't up for the job.

Dress nicely; come in clothing that is just a touch nicer than what you would wear day-to-day on the job. Make sure that you show up a little earlier so that you can come in on time and be calm and confident.

Eye Contact

This is extremely important, and the one thing that job candidates find difficult. The interviewer wants you to look them in the eye when you speak, and when they ask questions. If your eyes are constantly looking around the room, you may come off as uneasy, bored, or lying. You don't want to come off seeming like you want a staring contest, but normal eye contact during the exchange can help to create a connection.

Are You Real?

Whether you have come up with the answers or are answering spontaneously or are telling them the real story or what you think they want to hear, the interviewer wants you to be 100% familiar with how well matched you are for the position. Use your truthful answers to create a picture of the best possible match. Too often, candidates only share the part of their story that they think the interviewer wants to hear. This causes you to come off sounding phony.

Understand Your Weaknesses

"Hire an attitude, not just experience and qualification." – Greg Savage

Interviewers don't want to hear things like, "My biggest weakness is that I work too hard." That's not a weakness, and nobody is perfect. Interviewers know this, and they want to find people who can learn from their shortcomings and have figured out how to work around them. Make sure you know how to talk about two or three real weaknesses, and how you can overcome them.

Self-Starter

While they want to make sure that you can work well with others, they also want to know that you aren't going to sit around and twiddle your thumbs, waiting to be told what to do. They will look for clues that you can work independently, while also respecting coworkers and the company's management structure.

Flexibility and Adaptability

Employers like to ask behavioral questions, where interviewers will ask how you handled certain situations in the past, to see how your abilities are when it comes to adapting to new situations with success and ease. If you have job stories that show you can quickly solve problems, you will show them that you are a person who can rise to the occasion.

Reasonable Expectations

Not only is the employer looking to see if you are going to be a good fit, but they also want to know that the job is a good fit for you. Having an unhappy employee is not going to help anybody, and the hiring manager isn't going to want to have to go through the hiring process soon after.

While the majority of employers want you to be interested in growing vertically and horizontally within the company, it is important that you show them you know what the position is and isn't. They want to know how quickly you expect to advance, and to make sure that expectation is reasonable.

Respect for Management

The hiring manager wants somebody that fits into the company and respects management, as well as the culture and mission of the company. If you answer with stories about how you are smarter than management and always save the day, you are not going to come across very well. Even if the management in your last position was terrible, always share stories in a way that makes you come off as capable and resourceful, while not putting others down.

High Maintenance Personality

"Hire character. Train skill." – Peter Schultz

Some candidates walk in with complaint written all over their face from not getting to bring their parents or having to wait too long. Or, they emailed and called every day leading up to the interview asking questions. These are not good signs.

During the interview, the way a person shares a story will show if they expect a lot from others, in a bad way, and view things from their point of view and nobody else's. The company wants somebody willing to pitch in and help when need be.

Problem Solver

"Recently, I was asked if I was going to fire an employee who made a mistake that cost the company $600,000. No, I replied, I just spent $600,000 training him. Why would I want somebody to hire his experience?" – Thomas John Watson Sr.

Managers love problem solvers. Of course, you want to show that you wait until you have gathered up all of the facts and make sure that there is a problem that needs solving. Some people come into an interview with plans on how to fix a business, positive that these ideas are going to help them get the job. Having stories about how you fixed problems in previous positions are a good thing. Going into the interview to try to fix a company that you don't work for is not good.

Don't Be Too Eager

While employers do like candidates who are enthusiastic about the position, you can end up coming off as too enthusiastic. Being too enthusiastic can make you appear overly needy, and this makes you look bad. This will lower your chances of being hired. For example, if you are currently working somewhere else and you tell them that you can start right away, this could hurt your chances of getting the job. This shows them that you are willing to make an unprofessional exit from your current job by leaving without notice. The interviewer will start questioning if you are the right person for their team.

While it is a good idea to send a thank you after you have an interview, following up too much can hurt your chances. Emailing or calling them several times to check in on the status will only cause you to come off as desperate and is going to get on their nerves.

Do You Have The Skills?

You should have checked out the job description long before your interview, and you should have found examples of the skills you have that match what they want. Some companies have individual tests or interviews to check for these things, so make sure you are ready. If there is something that they want that you haven't done in a while, make sure you brush up on it before the interview.

Ask Them Questions

"When you hire people that are smarter than you are, you prove that you are smarter than they are." – RH Grant

A job interview is not a one-way street. The interviewer wants to see that you are interested in learning about them. This shows that you care about what work you do and whom you work for, instead of taking anything you can get. Asking them questions ensures that the people, position, and company is a good fit for what you want for yourself.

Make sure you go into the interview with three to five questions ready to ask them when given a chance. Some questions that you can ask the interviewer are:

> • What resources or staff support will I have to reach the department's goals?
>
> • What are the main priorities this position needs to accomplish within the next six months?
>
> • What is the culture like here?
>
> • In the last year, what has been the position's biggest challenge?
>
> • What caused this position to open?

These questions show the interviewer that you want to be successful, and they appreciate when you show this type of interest.

Why Mistakes Can Cost You the Job

Interviews are an important time to make sure you shine, but they are also important for the company. Making the wrong choice for an employee can bring devastating results. That is why a simple mistake can cost you the job. To help you understand why the interview process is so important, we are going to look at what it costs a company when they hire the wrong person.

The people that a company hires are the biggest factor when it comes to the success and growth that the company will experience. Employees are not only the people who deal with customers regularly, but they are also essential parts of the machine when it comes to providing needed services and delivering goods. When a business does not have a core team of effective and quality employees, it is impossible for them to stand apart, create a brand, and make their own customer experience.

During the hiring process, it isn't all about finding that person who can immediately fill the position—like a person who may not fit all of the requirements. It is important that they dedicate the resources and time needed to fill the position with someone who is dedicated to creating long-term success for the business. Employees are the most valuable and important asset to a company. Without employees, the business will cease to exist because no business is going to operate successfully and efficiently.

Everybody hired by a company brings along something unique, and it is important for employers to seek out people who have the best qualities. Not only do they end up wasting time not making the best decision during the hiring process, but they also lose a lot of financial resources on that bad fit.

According to some estimates, it can cost over a quarter of a million dollars to find and hire somebody. If they end up being the wrong person for the role, add to this the toll that the bad hire takes on their colleagues and managers, plus a whole host of other costs if they have to be replaced.

While most businesses know they need to make the best choice first, many of them do not use the resources they should, up front, to avoid this problem. A bad hire has a ripple effect among everybody within the business and the quality of the services.

Most businesses have, at some point, hired a person who ended up not being a good fit. There are many different things that HR can do to make sure that they don't waste their time recruiting, interviewing, and offering jobs to the wrong person.

The Cost of the Wrong Person

According to Jorgen Sundberg, CEO of Link Humans, the cost of recruiting, hiring, and training new hires can cost as much as $240,000. If that person turns out to be a bad fit, there are extra costs the business incurs, not the least of which is having to find their replacement. Brandon Hall Group discovered several variables that can play a part in coming up with the cost to replace bad hires. These include:

- Litigation fees
- Weakened employer brand

- Outplacement services

- Lost consumers

- Disruptions to projects that haven't been finished

- Negative impact on performance

- Training and relocation fees for replacements

- Staff time and advertisement fees for recruitment

The Effects of Bad Recruiting

When recruitment is done badly, there are many negative impacts that a business can suffer. Here are a few:

- *A bad candidate can reduce future job applications* – When there is a bad candidate experience, it can disillusion candidates. This disillusionment can cause a company to lose out on the opportunity to hire future people. 42% of people who responded to a CareerBuilder survey said that they decided never to seek employment from a company after a bad hire experience. 22% of people also said that they would not refer their colleagues or friends to the business either. It also causes the company to be less likely to get job applications from people who have read through the negative reviews on social media accounts by those disillusioned employees or candidates.

- *The added costs that are related to replacing the miss-hires* – These bad hires will either quit prematurely or be let go. Besides all of the obvious recruiting replacement costs or the costs that result from the hiring manager having to spend more time on recruiting instead of what their regular job is, the most significant revenue cost comes from not having any productivity in the role during the business day while it is vacant. If this vacant position is a revenue-generating position, the revenue you could have made during those vacant days can't be replaced. And even if it's not a revenue-generating position, the vacancy means that all of the other employees will be stressed more because they will have to do more work to fill in this gap. To make things worse, if recruiting ends up taking a long time to fill the position, the cost of this open place will increase dramatically.

• *Hiring a bad employee can reduce the power of the company's product brand* – At many businesses, it is hard to separate the employer brand and the product brand. For example, Google and Apple are one and two on product and employer brand. With this interconnection of the two, if the employer brand gets damaged, so does the product brand. So if the employer brand gets hurt by hiring a person with inexperience or due to a questionable hiring process, it can end up hurting the product brand and the sales it could create. These relationships between the brands are growing every day as social media sites, such as Glassdoor, continue to grow. It is straightforward for people and customers to learn about a negative employee or candidate experience, and then they use that to change their purchase decisions and job search. It's crazy, but any function that could indirectly hurt a company's product brand will guarantee a lower budget and a rough time in the corporation.

• *Lower productivity* – When a company has a weak employer brand, it will cause lower-quality hires in every job that gets filled. This is proven through the data from the Corporate Executive Board because they show that with a strong employer brand, the quality of your hires will increase by 9%. A weak recruiting process that constantly hires underqualified people is going to lower productivity, especially from the employee. For example, a bid hire works 10% below average, multiply the 10% by the average revenue per employee, and this will show the estimated cost of hiring just one person that works below average. If Apple were to hire one below average employee, it would cost them $240,000 in revenue.

• *Lowered revenue in positions that have a revenue impact* – When below average performers are hired in important revenue-generating and sales jobs, it can result in a huge reduction in revenue. There are also negative revenue impacts on several other revenue-impacted jobs, such as customer service and product development, as a result of bad performance due to below average hires in these roles. Bad hiring will cause less innovation when it comes to products and bad customer service once a sale has been made.

• *Lower product sales* – When there is a bad candidate experience, it frustrates and upsets other candidates. A large portion of these disillusioned candidates will strike back by not purchasing the company's retail products. Due to this disillusionment, it will cost the company product sales of 23% from candidates who, if they had a positive experience, would have been more likely to purchase services or products from them. It will also cost them sales from 9% of the candidate's friends and colleagues that they urge not to buy from the company. This means that it is crucial for the business to find out if the people they are interviewing are current customers and then to make sure that the company is responsive if they choose not to move forward with them.

Why Does This Still Happen?

If it is so time-consuming and expensive to hire the wrong person, why does this still happen?

CareerBuilder believes that one reason why companies hire the wrong person is that they rush to fill an open position. They performed a survey in 2012 asking why companies make bad hires; they discovered that 43% made a bad hire when they felt they had to pick somebody quickly.

This urgency can be created in many different ways. This includes: an important role in the company that needs urgent attention, a project might need a new talent, an important employee has suddenly left, or the current staff may be overextended. Hiring managers are often left feeling anxious about putting a person in a vacant spot that they often overlook the flaws of a candidate and end up hiring a person who does not meet the needs of the company.

22% of the respondents of the CareerBuilder survey felt that they lacked the skills necessary to hire and interview people. When it comes to hiring the wrong person, it shouldn't be the person hired that gets blamed; instead, it is the person who did the hiring that made the wrong choice. Hiring managers have to know what to look for during the hiring process.

What Is Needed to Hire the Right Person?

The first step in hiring the right person is making sure that the company has the right type of person leading the hiring process who is well informed of what the business needs. Talking with the executives and hiring manager about the needs of the business can help to make sure that a better decision is made.

This is why most companies have a standardized interview process. This provides them with the tools and questions to help them evaluate candidates. Peer-to-peer interviews and behavioral interviews help hiring managers to determine if a person would be a good fit for the company. This process works the same for every person that has applied for a job with the company. Those in charge of the hiring process are trained to spot any red flags during the interview process.

The process is meant to help people become relaxed before asking them questions that are worded in such a way that allows the interviewer to learn more about the person.

Almost a tenth of the survey respondents said that their bad hires did not work out because they didn't fully understand the company's culture or brand. This is why it is important for a company to make sure that they have a clear brand, and the prospective employee should do plenty of research to learn more about the company.

Common Mistakes Made When Applying for a Job

Before you get a job interview, you have to apply for the job. If this is not done successfully, then you will never get to shine for the hiring manager and convince them to hire you.

While the ultimate goal for everybody is to get a job, the way everybody approaches this will vary, and several questions exist when it comes to strategy. For example, are you going to browse through online listings or are you going to use a newspaper? Are you planning on calling up the people you know within a specific field to help you find some possible leads or are you going to try to find things on your own? How much of a role do social media sites, such as LinkedIn, going to play?

The hardest part of finding a job is figuring out what it is that you want to do. Having a degree in a particular field or working several years in a certain industry shouldn't limit all of your options. It isn't uncommon for a person to have five or more different careers during their life. It may come off as cliché, but every day of your life you will learn something new about your likes and dislikes and strengths and weaknesses.

When you are picking a career or changing one, there are two questions that you need to think about.

First, while a certain job or industry may look enticing, are you prepared to do what it requires day in and day out? You have to ask yourself whether you are going to want to meet all of the demands of the job or if you think it is something that is going to impress your friends.

Second, are you ready to live the life the job requires? For example, while being a personal assistant to a celebrity might sound like a dream job, are you willing to be at their beck and call all day? Are you going to be able to withstand belittling comments and a possible difficult personality? High-paying or high-profile jobs won't give you much in the way of free time. If you aren't familiar with the primary duties of a position, try to talk to somebody else that is in the field or a career counselor so that you can learn as much as possible. You need to do a lot of research into the job, what it requires, and the company before ever accepting it. What you think might be a dream job could end up being a nightmare.

Career planning is a science all on its own, and you shouldn't feel weird to ask for help from professionals when it comes to figuring out where to go next. If you are still in college, there are probably plenty of these professionals in your school's career planning office. If you are familiar with the workforce, there are many career planning centers in your community. Do some research and set up an appointment to meet with one. Some career planners do work virtually, which will allow you to connect with planners that aren't in your area.

Career Tests

If you are not sure what you want to do, career tests are an excellent way for you to learn more about your career possibilities and preferences. Most tests are available through trade and industry associations and most commonly available online. Many of these associations publish magazines that will provide you with insights into a particular career. It might be a good idea to take some time to investigate a job more.

If you do not have the time to meet up with a career professional, there are online sites that can help you research types of careers that could work for you. Some people thing career tests are stupid or a waste of time, but they can be helpful. Since it is true that a career professional, pre-manufactured form, or computer doesn't know you better than you know you, you shouldn't solely rely on what these things tell you. However, try to keep an open mind; if there is something the test says might be a good idea that you have never thought about, take a few minutes to read up on it. You never know; it might be your dream career.

Employers will also sometimes use career tests as part of the screening process, and it can be helpful if you are already familiar with some of the most common tests used. These include:

- CAPS – Career Ability Placement Test

CAPS is a timed test. It may not tell you whether the answers were right or wrong, but it does give you an indication of how you scored in eight areas of language usage, verbal reasoning, spatial relations, and mechanical reasoning.

- MBTI – Myers Brigs Type Indicator

Using the MBTI has started to become popular in figuring out if a candidate will fit into a company's culture. MBTI measures a person's personality in four areas: judging/perceiving, sensing/intuitive, thinking/feeling, and extrovert/introvert.

- SII – Strong Interest Inventory

The SII measures a person's interests based on their answers about different activities that fall into six categories: realistic, enterprising, artistic, conventional, investigative, and social. The SDS, or Self-Directed Search, is similar to SII. It focuses on the same areas, but it is a shorter test.

Recruiters and Counselors

Recruiters and counselors have become very popular among job seekers over the past few years. With the increasing number of applicants, it has made effective and experienced counselors important brokers of employers and positions. Recruiters and counselors are not only able to help a person save time by working through the process of sifting through jobs and applicants, but they can also offer professional advice to applicants so that they can find what it is that they are looking for and help them sell themselves more effectively.

Now, you may be wondering what the difference is between a recruiter and counselor. You know those advertisements on web pages? Those were put there by recruiters. These recruiters could be an employee of the company that is looking to hire somebody, or they are a third party that has been contracted by the company. If it is the latter, then there was probably a fee involved—but that is typically paid for by the company looking to hire.

If you head to a career coach or counselor, you will handle any costs that are required, unless it is an outplacement service that your former employer or college is offering. Career counselors do not help you find a job; instead, they help you figure out the type of job you need to look for. If the job market confuses you, a career counselor is there to help you to clarify your career goals and aim you in the best direction. You have to watch out for the type of contract you sign. Some counselors insist on being paid first, and their fees can be as high as $2,000 to $15,000. You want to find a counselor who has Master Career Counselor credentials, state licensure, and charges by the hour. A great way to find a counselor is to check out ncda.org.

The following are some helpful tips when it comes to working with counselors and recruiters:

- Respond to any inquiries made by counselors or recruiters if they reach out to you, even if you have no interest in the position. This will put you on their radar, and you want to be there to make a good impression because there could be another position that opens up in the future that you do want.

• Keep in touch with them to build rapport and stay in their mind when new jobs come up.

• Be upfront about your job goals and expectations. This includes the things you are interested in and what you aren't.

• Don't double dip. If you have already been in contact with one recruiter for a certain position and then another one gets in touch with you, be truthful with them about your other relationship.

• Feel free to let counselors and recruiters know that you want what you talk about and all your information to remain confidential. While most of them automatically work this way, it is best to say something to make sure that you are both on the same page.

Techniques for Job Seeking

There are many different ways to try to find a job. Some of them include:

• Sending out resumes to employers that are unsolicited, also referred to as the direct contact method.

• Calling a personal contact, also known as networking. You can ask other professionals how they ended up getting their current position, and there are going to be some that say they got their job through a business contact, family member, or friend. No matter what your profession is, the chances are that you probably know somebody in that field already or at least somebody who knows somebody. Either way, you should be able to locate somebody in the field who can help you out. Even if they aren't able to offer you a job, they may be able to aim you in the right direction. Making connections are a great way to get into a new career field and advance your career.

If you haven't been able to locate somebody who can help, there are many other ways to make contacts. Try to find local organizations that specialize in what you do and make a point of attending their meetings. You can also contact your college's alumni association and see if you can find another graduate who is in that field. You can also go online and engage with some other professionals on job boards. While you may not get offers right away, don't be surprised if you end up hearing from some of these contacts later on about new opportunities.

• Getting help from an employment service firm or recruiter. If you have no time to pore through the classifieds, actively look through job postings, or print up a resume and cover letters, employment services can help. Whether you want a direct-hire job or a temporary job, there are plenty of staffing firms to help service what the job seeker needs, whether executive or entry-level.

But what exactly do they do? They do whatever it is that you want them to do. They can be specialized in what they do, or general. They may offer one specific service that helps a small group of job seekers, or they may provide a large number of services to help a large number of people.

If you want to have a staffing firm help you out, don't pick one blindly. The National Association of Personnel Services and the American Staffing Association are two great choices that will uphold ethical business practices. They do require a membership though.

• Answering a help-wanted advertisement. While seeing the words "Help Wanted" probably makes you think of the classified pages in a newspaper, that is by no means the only place to find help-wanted ads. With technology, there are now literally thousands of websites that are for job hunters. You can access millions of job openings from around the world with just a couple of clicks. Professional and trade organizations are a perfect place for information about profession-specific jobs. Magazines are a great place to look for job listings, which can also be accessed online.

Resume Mistakes

Now you have gone through the process of trying to find a job to apply to, the next thing you have to do is get an interview by creating an attention-grabbing resume.

Your resume is what employers read to get to know your skills and decide if they want to spend the time and energy to bring you in for an interview. This is why you have to make sure that your resume has as much detail and information as possible, without going beyond the one-page limit. Another function of the resume is to be attractive and draw as much attention your way as possible. The only way to get a job offer is to get noticed. Very few people still send out hard copy resumes through the US mail. Instead, this process is being replaced by online recruitment techniques, which will sometimes give you the chance to attach a file. In some other cases, you will have to fill out online forms that are going to be different depending on the position and company.

- Unsolicited Resumes

A huge frustration that job seekers have to face is looking through a company's open positions and not finding a spot that works for them. What should happen if your dream company isn't hiring people? Send them your resume anyway!

Most people think about sending their resume to human resources, but you should think beyond HR. Get in touch with line managers. They are the ones who usually make the hiring decisions. See if you can get the name of a person in the department that you would like to work in. At best, try to start a dialogue so that you can get a good idea as to what they want. At worst, they will push you back towards HR.

There are also many companies who will provide you with a chance to sign up for notifications about job openings in your area of interest. You can also do this through recruitment websites like Monster. The resume is what stands between you and an interview. Most jobs are going to try to hire within first before posting a job opening—this saves them time and money. However, if they are unable to find somebody within the company to fill the position, and they already have your resume, you may be getting a call. That being said, if you have a bad resume, it will likely see the trashcan.

Let's take a look at some of the worst resume mistakes so that you can make sure to avoid them:

1. Grammatical errors and typos

This may be the most obvious thing, but your resume needs to be grammatically perfect. If it's not, the employer is going to reach some unflattering conclusions about you, such as "They don't care," or "They can't write."

2. Lacks specifics

The resume shouldn't have the obvious written on it. Employers want to understand the things that you have accomplished. Things like:

"I worked with employees in a restaurant."

"I recruited, hired, trained, and managed over twenty employees in a restaurant that made $2 million in sales annually."

These phrases can describe the same person, but the second one grabs your attention with its specifics.

3. Using the one-size-fits-all resume

When you try to come up with a generic resume to send out to every ad you see, you can almost guarantee that they are going to throw it in the trash. With the lack of effort, you come off like, "I'm not interested in the job. Frankly, any job is fine."

Employers need to feel special, and they want to receive a resume that has been made especially for them. They want you to clearly state how and why you will fit into their open position and organization.

4. Showing duties and not accomplishments

You want your resume to show how good you are at what you can do, but it's really easy to fall into the trap of listing your duties. Things like: updated files, worked with children, or recorded minutes at meetings are boring.

That reiterates the job description. Employers are more interested in the things that you accomplished than the things you did. Add more details so that you have something like this:

"Reorganized ten years of files to make them easily accessible to the department."

"Created three activities for preschool children and helped them create a ten-minute holiday program."

"Recorded weekly meeting minutes and create a Microsoft Word file for future reference."

5. Cutting things short or going on

Despite some of the things that you may have heard, there aren't any actual rules for the length of the resume. Why? Because people who have different expectations and preferences when it comes to resumes are going to be reading it.

This doesn't mean that you can send out five-page resumes. Generally speaking, if you can't say it in one, don't go over two. One is the best though. However, make sure that you don't cut too much good stuff out of your resume to try to get it to fit into a one-page standard.

6. Bad summary

Employers will read over your career summary, but they will often look over information that is fluff. Give them specifics and information that focuses on what they need.

7. No action verbs

Don't say things like, "I was responsible for…" Instead, add in some action verbs. These words show your initiative and punch up the tone of the resume. Try, "I developed a new onboarding program for new hires."

8. Left off important info

You might find yourself tempted to leave out jobs that you took to earn money for school. However, the soft skills that you learned throughout these jobs are more important than you might think.

9. Too much going on

If you have used a bunch of different fonts on your resume, it is going to give the person reading it a headache. Ask some friends to look at your resume to see if you have too much going on. If it's hard on their eyes, then you should probably redesign it.

10. Bad contact info

You could have the best resume in the world, but if the person can't contact you, then you won't be getting an interview. They aren't going to go out of their way to get the correct email or phone number. Double-check your contact information and make sure everything is correct.

Cover Letter Mistakes

The next thing employers are going to look at is your cover letter. These do not necessarily help you in the initial selection process; they can help make you stand out from the competition in later rounds. When responding to a classified advertisement, make sure that you use some of the keywords that the ad used.

Make sure you take the time to put together a letter for each application you send in. Like the resume, they want to know it is meant for them and not some generic cover letter that you make a couple of address changes to. Also, before going further into cover letter mistakes, make sure it is grammatically correct.

1. Focusing too much on you

Companies hire people to do things for them. This means that they would like to learn what you can do for them. While you should touch on your accomplishments, make sure you also explain why you can fill the void in their company.

2. Sharing information from every job you've ever had

Depending on how many jobs you've had, this could mean a very confusing and crowded cover letter. Instead of sharing about every job you've had, share what experiences relate to the position. Create a cover letter that talks about those skills instead of giving them your life story.

3. Sharing something uncomfortable

You don't want to share recent struggles you have faced in your cover letter. The person reading it isn't interested in why you were fired or laid off. This is going to be seen as a red flag. These things can be addressed in the interview if need be.

4. Writing a novel

Cover letters rarely get read, but have a novel-like cover letter is going to annoy many hiring managers. The majority of hiring managers prefer cover letters to be half a page or less.

5. Rehashing the resume

They already know your resume; they read that first. They aren't going to want to read back through it when it comes to your cover letter.

6. Being trite

Be specific in the things you can provide to their company. Avoid statements like, "I believe I am the best fit..."

Claiming Skills You Don't Have or Lying

As you may have noticed, lying wasn't mentioned in the last two sections. That was because it gets to have its own section because it is probably the worst thing that you can do when applying for a job. It's also something that you will see more of later in the book.

While you may feel tempted to embellish your application to increase your chances of getting an interview, doing so is a huge risk. Many consequences come with these lies.

There are several types of lies that a person can make on their resume or application. It can be a slight embellishment of the truth to extreme lies. Dates might be changed a bit to try and add gaps in employment. Achievements might be embellished a bit. There can be an overinflation of skill. Some people have even claimed work experience or degrees that they have never possessed. When it comes to legal issues of these lies, a company looks to see if it was "material" or not. This means if it could potentially influence a person's decision.

If you pay attention to the application process, there will probably be a disclaimer that says the information is needed to help assess a person's qualifications for a position. It continues by saying that if a person knowingly lies about this information, it is grounds for termination. If the application doesn't say this, most employers will still use their rights to fire a now-employee for omissions or lies during the application process.

Most states have at-will employment laws. All this means is that a person can leave their job whenever they want. It also implies that their employer has the right to terminate their employment relationship whenever they want unless their reason is illegal. If you get fired for lying on an application, it can cause a never-ending cycle. That means you have to tell the truth about them firing you for your next job application or you will risk omitting information, again.

When you lie during the application process, you also run the risk of losing your right to sue the employer if you have any legal claims, such as termination due to racial discrimination. That is what is known as the "after-acquired evidence" rule. It means that they can use whatever evidence they learned about you in defense against your legal claim. Their position is that if you had told the truth on the application, they wouldn't have hired you in the first place. They will have to prove your lies, how they were linked to your position and were enough for them not to have hired you.

If you are a licensed professional, lying during the job application can cost you your license.

It is not likely that you will face criminal charges for lying on the application, but some circumstances could cause criminal charges. For example, if you lie about military service to get some form of benefit, you can be prosecuted through the Stolen Valor Act. If you are applying for a federal or state job, you will probably face charges because you will have lied to a state or federal government agent.

Most white lies aren't going to cause a fraud charge, but fraud charges can be brought against you if the effect of the lie caused damage to the financial welfare of a business or a person.

You could also face civil liabilities. For example, if an architect lied about their credentials, they could be civilly liable for misrepresentation or civil fraud if a part of a building collapsed and hurt somebody.

The problems list is endless when it comes to not telling the truth on a job application. Plus, it sticks with you. It can make getting another job virtually impossible.

Not Being Creative or Unique

After you have taken the time to create your resume, it would be nice to think that you are all done. You have made sure that there aren't any spelling errors, it's not busy, and you feel ready to send it out.

The problem is: HR doesn't want to receive the same resume from everybody. They do not want to see a Word document template; they want something unique and creative.

The good news is that you don't have to write a new resume or cover letter for every single application. You can create a master copy of both with all of your certifications, skills, and experiences. Then, you can go in and make small changes to them for each job you are applying for so that they are all unique.

Now, there are some instances where changing your resume and cover letter completely will boost your chances of getting an interview. One instance will be if you have a job listing that you are extremely excited about. Go the extra mile with these. Customize your resume to show the types of things that the employer wants to see.

Another instance will be if you are making a career more. If you have worked as a sales representative for a while, and you want to change to an account manager, you are going to need to change your resume to show how the skills you have would work in the new position.

Yes, this might slow down your job application process, but once you get the hang of things, it will become easier. Plus, you will likely receive more interview calls.

Not Being True to Yourself and Your Skills

Employers need to know you, and you need to know that you are going to like the job. That is why it is so important that you make sure you are true to yourself and your skills.

Applying for a job that you are overqualified for is going to send off warning signs with the employer. Before we talk about that, let's talk about what it means for you. Are you going to be happy working 40 hours a week at a job where you will be doing things that are likely very easy for you to accomplish? Sure, it might easily work, but are you not going to get bored and tired of doing things that you could do in your sleep?

Now, as far as the employer is concerned, you could come off as desperate or unconfident. They are either going to think that you are in such a desperate need of a job that you are willing to take anything, or you are unsure of yourself and your skills. Either way, it is not going to make them want to hire you. They want somebody who is going to enjoy coming into work every day and who is completely confident in their abilities.

On the flip side of things, if you apply for a job that you are underqualified for, it is going to send off similar red flags for the employer. This is going to make you appear arrogant. It could also make them think that you are not paying attention, or just browsing through the job board applying to every job you see and not paying attention to what each one requires.

When you are applying for a job, you have to make sure that you are qualified for the job and would be happy doing the work. Employers want people who know themselves, who know what makes them happy, and what they want to do. They do not want to spend a ton of time training them in something they don't know anything about or worrying that they are going to quit because the work isn't challenging enough.

Show them that you know yourself.

Common Mistakes Before the Interview

You got your resume ready and a perfect cover letter. Companies are looking for someone who has experience, skills, and can fit into the company culture. They want to see if your ideas and personality will complement the people you will be working with. There are many ways you can let the interviewer know that you are the person.

Preparation

Getting ready for an interview takes patience and time. It is not something you can do ten minutes before you leave for your interview. It is something that you can learn, and it gets easier each time you do it. You start learning what questions will be asked and can figure out what answers will work best. The more interviews you have, the closer you will be to getting that perfect job.

The part that takes the most time is researching your prospective employer. It is also the most important part. The best way to show you are the best candidate is leaving a positive impression with the interviewer. The best way to do this is by knowing all the aspects of the company. You shouldn't do this early in the job search. You need to wait until you have been asked to come in for an interview.

- Finding the information

There are many tools and ways you can find the information you need. The first one is fairly obvious: knowing someone inside the company. If you don't know anyone, you might be able to create a contact. You might have a relative or friend that knows somebody that works at the company and can help you out.

You also need to find information about the company's competitors. There is a whole lot of information at local libraries, in magazines, newspapers, and journals. Focus on stats. Focus on companies who are in the same field as the one you are interviewing with. Take a close look at the ones who are leading the field. A few facts about them can help you during the interview.

Look for everything. Find enough information to be able to do a ten-minute presentation. Find as many facts as possible so you can talk intelligently about the company. You have to know what kind of services and products they offer, the customers they deal with, the business and name of their parent company, and businesses and names of any subsidiaries. Find out where they rank in the industry, profit and sales trends, type of ownership, size, and whatever else seems important to you. Learn the company jargon. If you know who will be conducting the interview, do some research on them too.

- Doing internet research

There are many places online where you can find information effectively and quickly. The first place to begin is the company's website. In addition to fundamental information, you need to find their history, mission statement, list of executives, and annual reports. If they have press releases, read the latest one. This shows the interviewer you know what is happening in the company. Many sites will give you facts you should know about an industry.

- Getting the most out of research

  o Look for online discussions where employees or experts discuss the company. This type of commentary may give you insight into the value and culture of the company.

o Read news reports and releases about what the company is feeling. Reports are more objective and give insight into how executives manage. Looking into third-party sources might give you insight into troubling information about the financial health of the company that might help you stay away from a sinking ship.

o Try not to restrict your search to just the newest listings. Some older postings might not have been filled and might have less competition since many job searchers only focus on the newest postings.

o Use the company's website to learn about certain careers. This information is probably being used by many companies and might be more general than more specific requirements that most companies look for. This can help you get an understanding of the career you are interested in.

o Use social media opportunities. Contacts on Facebook and LinkedIn might work for companies you are connected to. Find employees within your online network. Get in touch with them to get the information you need about the company.

• Mock Interviews

Sit down with some good friends that you trust and have some mock interviews. Have them ask you questions and see how well you can answer them. Ask for their honest feedback. Did you sound confident and assured? Were your answers off the mark or rambling? Would they hire the person that answered the questions? If not, then you need to do some work.

Have them record the interview so you can look at yourself through the eyes of the interviewer. Watch your body language since it tells you a lot about yourself. Were you slouching? Were you attentive and sitting up straight? Did you keep eye contact without staring? Your body language needs to show the interviewer that you are focused and alert. Do not cross your legs or fold your arms. Your hands can work against you as well. If you gesture when you talk, you need to get that under control. Keep your hands folded in your lap. If you take the time to work on all the above, you will be well on your way to a great interview.

- Phone Screen

Some companies will do a phone interview before they bring you in for an in-person interview. At this point, they already know that you meet all of their basic requirements. This pre-interview is simply their way of determining if you are worth their time to set up an in-person interview or continue with the process.

To be honest, phone interviews are not great because most people are never prepared for them, and people will often do a bad job of putting their best foot forward. Most of the time, it is because they don't give credit to how important the phone interview is.

There are three main reasons why companies will choose to do a phone interview:

1. They want to learn that you can perform certain tasks. They are looking for you to validate what you said that you could do. This is where you want to jump ahead of the competition by talking about your accomplishments and work experience. Then you want to take things a step further by providing them with a vision of what you can help them do.

2. They want to find out that you want the position. Nobody is interested in wasting their time interviewing somebody

who isn't interested in the job. You need to show them that you are passionate about your line of work.

3. They want to find out if they like you. You can have some of the best experience, and it could mean nothing to them if they don't think that you would be a great leader and a good team player. There have been plenty of hiring authorities who have chosen to "pass" on a candidate who had amazing qualifications. They pass on doing an in-person interview because they didn't want to waste their time meeting somebody who has a bad personality and poor leadership skills.

When getting ready for your phone interview, make sure that you have your resume with you. Most people think that this isn't necessary because the interviewer already knows their work history. No! Have your resume with you.

It is a known fact that during phone interviews—no matter how experienced the person is—the interviewee will get nervous or distracted and end up forgetting some of the most basic facts—like the correct name of an employer, detailed job descriptions, exact job titles, employment dates, and more. Plus, they will sometimes forget to ask their interviewer some important questions because they didn't have them written down in front of them. Here are some things you should make sure you do during a phone interview:

1. If possible, stand while talking with them. You can project your voice better, and this will make the conversation more engaging.

2. As stated earlier, have your questions and resume with you.

3. Ask what stage they are at in the interview process, and try to find out what was lacking from the other applicants that they have talked to. This shows that you have great leadership skills. This will give you a way to place yourself

ahead of the competition, and it will also engage the interviewer more, so you have a conversation with them instead of an interview.

4. You need to help the interviewer paint an accurate picture of you. Let your personality come through. Ask questions, laugh, be engaging. They have no clue who you are, and they are trying to create a picture of you as best they can without having to meet you in person.

5. If you are very interested in the job, invite yourself for an in-person interview once the phone interview has come to an end.

Let's take a look at how to invite yourself to an in-person interview. It may sound daunting, but it is very easy to do. This works because the interviewer will either validate their interest and set up another meeting or will be forced to tell you why they aren't interested in going forward with you at this time. Either way, you will know where you are on their radar and won't be left wondering.

As the phone interview comes to an end, once you have thanked them for the call, say, "I am very much interested in the job. I feel that my qualifications fit your needs, and I would like to get to meet with you for an in-person interview." Then, stop talking. Wait for them to respond.

They will either comply and set up an in-person interview or will say something along the lines of, "We are still in the process of screening other applicants. We will get in contact with you if we are interested."

If they show that they aren't interested, you may want to say something like, "Are you concerned about my qualifications?" This might get you a direct and honest answer, or not—but it's not going to hurt anything to ask. However, only ask this if it is apparent that they are concerned about your abilities to perform the job well; otherwise, this could end up doing more harm than good.

In the end, phone interviews are critical. They are somewhat more important than the in-person interview because if things do not go well, you won't get the in-person interview.

What to Bring

When it comes to an interview, they are about 80% preparation and 20% execution. We've already talked about different ways to prepare for your interview by using mock interviews and other practice tips. Now, let's look at how to make sure that you have everything that you need for your interview.

Let's take a moment to picture a scenario. You step into the office of your dream job, shake the hiring manager's hand, sit down, and then realize you have forgotten everything at home. You have no copies of your resume, no paper or pen to take notes with—it's a miracle that you put on deodorant.

Unfortunately, this lack of prep can end up costing you the job. To make sure that this doesn't happen, you should start preparing for the interview as soon as the interview has been set up.

Here are some things that you have to make sure you bring with you when you go to your interview, so you're 100% prepared:

1. Folder

You will no doubt have paperwork for the interview, so a folder is a great place to store all of these documents. This will show that you are organized. This is a soft skill that many employers are looking for.

2. Copies of your resume

Yes, you should have more than one copy of your resume with you. The chances are that you had already sent in a copy of your resume when you applied, but don't assume that the interviewer will have the copy on hand. They are busy people, so they may have forgotten to print it to bring with them.

Why do you need more than one copy? You don't know how many people will be on the interview panel, and more likely than not, all of them will want to see a copy of your resume.

3. Business cards

While your resume should have all of your contact information on it, and the business card might seem a bit old school, it doesn't hurt to have them with you. They are small and easy to carry, and you never know if somebody might ask for you. That's why it is always good to have some handy.

4. Work samples or portfolio

If you work in a creative industry, such as fashion, architecture, design, journalism, or advertising, make sure to bring plenty of the work you have done in the past. You should offer to send them an electronic copy of your portfolio later on. Depending on your line of work, you might want to bring along a sheet that shows all of the positive feedback that you have received from previous clients.

5. References

When your interview goes well—because after all of this it will—and they ask you for your references on the spot, make sure that you have a list prepared with all of the referees' contact information. Theoretically, you should be able to email the company your reference information once you get home, but this is a wrong approach. You want the company to have everything that they need to move forward with the hiring process. Plus, it will make you look more efficient if you have come prepared.

6. Pen and paper

Taking notes during your interview can be helpful for many reasons. First, it shows that you are actively listening and engaged in the conversation, and it ensures that you won't end up forgetting important information about the job. Plus, you can refer back to these notes later on in order to send out a personalized thank you note.

Before you start taking notes, make sure you ask the interviewer if it is okay that you do so. Make sure that you don't take so many brief records that you are unable to make eye contact. Also, bring more than one pen in case one runs out of ink.

7. Questions

To show that you are genuinely interested in the position, you need to make sure that you have prepared some questions to ask them in advance that shows you understand the company's culture, challenges, and core values. The following are a few questions that you could ask:

- How do your managers provide feedback to the employees?

- What is done to help encourage collaboration and camaraderie among coworkers?

- What are the most important things that I could accomplish during my first 60 days on the job?

- How are successes defined and measured?

8. Talking points

Job interviews are stressful and nerve-wracking. One of the best ways to reduce stress before you go into the interview and to help build your confidence is to make sure that you can jog your memory by taking a look at some notes that you jotted down before the interview that you want to make sure were covered. These could be notes about things like anecdotes that highlight your strengths and accomplishments and other specific skills.

You can come up with a list, which is a summary of the accomplishments you have achieved that are organized by skill sets, that you can look at right before you go into your interview. You should make sure that these accomplishments match up with the job's responsibilities. For example, if your interview is for a management position, you will want to talk about the last project you oversaw and describe how the project succeeded.

9. Identification

This may seem like a no-brainer, but it still has to be mentioned. You might have to have photo ID to get into the building, so check with the hiring manager before the interview to find out what their security requirements are. You would hate for security to ask for ID and not have it with you. They also may ask you for the company's name you are visiting, the name of the person you're meeting with, and the floor that the meeting is on. Make sure that you confirm all of this information when the interview is set up to make sure that you are not left confused in the lobby before the interview.

10. Contact information and directions

You should make sure a day before the interview that you know where you are going. Still, on the day of, make sure that you have the address written down should you need to use your GPS. Also, make sure that you have the contact information for the company should you need to get in touch with them beforehand in case anything goes wrong.

11. Mint

While you don't want to be chewing gum during the interview, eating a piece beforehand might be a good idea to make sure that your breath is fresh. Alternatively, you can pop a breath mint right before you head in for the interview.

12. A smile

Most of the time, a smile might come off as corny, but smiling will make you look better to the interviewer. Employers want to know that you are excited and enthusiastic about the job.

There are some things that you shouldn't bring to the interview as well. Here are a few:

- Your parents—as strange as it seems, it happens

- Excessive jewelry

- Drinks

- Food

- Chewing gum

When you have all of the things gathered and ready to go for your interview, you can move on to the next step in the preparation process.

Dress Code

This sounds superficial, but people judge you by the way you dress. However, that doesn't mean you have to wear Prada. What you look like on the outside shows what you are on the inside. If the interviewer can see that you took the time to pick the right clothing, it tells them that you put the same amount into your work. If you go to your interview dressed too casually, you are telling the interviewer that you don't care about the company or job. Dress up a bit more than you usually would if you were going to work for the day. You should take into consideration the basic rules listed below:

- Men

If you are interviewing for a professional position, always wear a suit. Wearing a shirt and tie might be fine for your current job, but it won't cut it for an interview. Wear conservatives colors, such as charcoal gray, navy blue, or black. Flashy or bright colors will distract the interviewer, and they won't listen to you as closely.

You can easily jazz up a conservative suit by changing up the shirt or tie or even both. If you have one suit, changing these can help a lot if you are interviewing with companies that require more than one interview on different occasions. Stay away from shiny shirts too—they should only be worn in nightclubs. Make sure you wear socks that blend in with your pants and shoes.

- Women

The proper attire for women in the workplace has changed much over the past few decades. The power suit that used to rule the scene has been downgraded to a pantsuit that doesn't look much different than a man's. Women wearing pants is now more acceptable and might be more appropriate in jobs where you will be walking a lot or getting in and out of cars. If you wear a skirt, the length of the skirt should be professional and tasteful. Nothing shorter than knee length is appropriate. It doesn't matter what the company's dress code is; women are expected to wear a suit to the interview.

The colors need to be conservative. Navy blue or black pants or a skirt along with a jacket would be your best choice. Stay away from colors such as powder-blue or pink— they don't help you look professional. Never wear anything that dangles—this applies to necklaces, bracelets, and earrings. Lastly, stay away from clothing that fits too tight—you won't be comfortable, and the interviewer won't take you seriously.

- Grooming

Personal grooming is critical, and you have to take care of it before you head out the door. Careful grooming shows self-confidence and thoroughness. Women shouldn't wear too much makeup or jewelry. If you paint your fingernails, make sure it is a conservative color.

Men need to make sure their facial hair is trimmed and neat. If you have a mustache or beard, it needs to be well groomed. If not, make sure you're clean-shaven at the time of the interview. If you have an interview at four but your five o'clock shadow shows up at three, make sure you can get home for a quick shave before your interview.

All candidates need to wear little to no cologne or perfume. Clothes that smell like cigarette smoke might offend the interviewer if they have a sensitive nose. Take out any facial jewelry and cover tattoos with long sleeves. Put your water bottle into a briefcase and leave the backpack in the car.

Lateness

The person who called and asked you for an interview will ask you if you need directions to the building. NEVER refuse these directions. Even if you think you know their location, you need to know *exactly* where you are going.

If you are not familiar with that particular area, it is still a great idea to drive there before you have to go for the interview. Map out directions and see how long it is going to take you to get there. Even if you have a GPS, getting specific from a person who goes there all the time will give you more backup than the GPS.

Remember to add a few minutes for traffic or other unforeseen delays. Try to arrive at least ten to fifteen minutes early. When you schedule your interview, make sure you know who will be interviewing you. The person who calls to set up the interview isn't always the person who does the interviews. Ask their name, title, and phone number. Put this information into your cell phone to have available in case a problem comes up. This way, you can contact them directly.

- Arrival time

Just like other issues during the interview process, determining the right time to arrive is tricky. One rule you need to remember is being late, even "casually late", will never be acceptable. Lateness is one of the main reasons interviewers don't hire someone for the job. If there aren't any extenuating circumstances, you always need to arrive early. If there are circumstances, call the interviewer and tell them that you are going to be a bit late.

The best time to get to your interview is about ten to fifteen minutes early. Anything less and you will be cutting it close. If you get there too soon, you will look too anxious. Remember: you are also taking up other people's time. If might even be that if you arrive on time, the interviewer might not be ready to talk with you. When you do arrive, if you are told that it will be a few minutes, take this time to use the restroom, compose yourself, and wait patiently.

- Call ahead

Give the person doing the interview a call as soon as you realize you are going to be late. The sooner you get in front of the damage control, the better off you will be.

If you have inadvertently left the interviewer's number at home, call the company and let somebody there know. They should be able to pass your message on to the correct person. Just simply say, "Hi, my name is… I have an interview for the position of… at two p.m. I am running a bit late. I'll be there as soon as I can."

There might be some situations when calling ahead isn't possible— like you had a car accident. You are going to be preoccupied, and this is understandable. With that being said, do try to call the company and tell them at your earliest convenience.

- Apologize

If you have ever waited two hours for a friend to make their appearance to your dinner party, which you spent an entire week getting ready for, it will be safe to say that your frustration level will be over the top. Even more so if they don't apologize.

Now think about doing that to an employer who has taken 30 minutes out of their day to talk to you about your experience to see if you will be a good fit for the company. Even if you're only ten minutes late, you can, at the very least, acknowledge this and give them a sincere apology for messing up their day.

- Prove that you are adaptable

Think about this scene from the movie *The Pursuit of Happiness*:

Christopher Gardner drags himself into an interview; it is going to end up changing his life while he wears a tank top splattered with paint after he has spent the night in jail. Even though he isn't appropriately dressed, he professionally conducts himself and can impress his future bosses. Not only does he prove that he is better than his tattered outfit, but he also demonstrates that he is adaptable.

50% of any job interview is about the interviewer getting to know who you are as a person, and getting a good feel for how you are going to fit within the company. How you can handle yourself under the pressure of being late to your interview is going to say a lot about who you are and how you will conduct yourself if you get the job. If you end up being late to your job interview, there is a good chance that you might end up being late to a meeting with a client, and the company is interested to see how well you can recover. When you walk in late, it turns into a test of how well you can handle this unfortunate situation.

If you do find yourself in the uncomfortable position of showing up late to your interview, all might not be lost. Make sure you are prepared and work through the situation like a professional; you might end up saving the interview and your job opportunity.

- A good reason for being late

Most of the time, the interviewer isn't going to ask why you are late, but you need to give them a reason anyway. It needs to be a good one. "Sorry, I didn't hear the alarm" or "I'm stuck in traffic" isn't going to cut it. Neither is: "I'm having a bad day"; "My cat coughed up a hairball on my blouse"; "My washing machine flooded the floor"; "I left only to realize that I was wearing two different shoes"; and "I ran back inside to change my shoes and then my car wouldn't start."

Interviewers are not the unforgiving monsters that we think they are. They know that life happens. If the reason you are late to your interview is something that couldn't be avoided, like a family emergency or a flat tire, then don't make up silly excuses.

The thing to remember is to give them information. Honesty has always been the best way to go.

- Give them an arrival time

Sending an email or calling ahead is not going to do much if you don't tell them how soon you will be there. Just saying, "I'll be there as soon as possible" is nothing. This could mean ten minutes away, or the train hasn't left the station.

They aren't asking for an exact time, but you need to give them a good estimate. Making them sit there wondering where you are or when you will get there might be a deal breaker. You don't want that to happen.

When you give them your arrival time, try to figure out the amount of time you need actually to get there. Then add on about five minutes for a buffer. Never tell them you have added in buffer time.

- Get ready to reschedule

The interviewer has set this time aside to talk with you, and you probably aren't the only person they are talking to that day. Their time is just as valuable as yours.

When you call to let them know you are going to be late, you need to be prepared for them to reschedule or cancel the interview. They have other things to do than to cater to your needs.

What is worse is that they go ahead and talk with the other candidate who showed up extremely early for their interview. They did show up very early, but at least they showed up before the interview's scheduled time.

- Take a moment to get yourself composed

Once you finally make it to the interview, it is imperative that you take a few moments to compose yourself before heading to the reception desk.

You might already be late, but taking a few minutes to check your appearance can make all the difference. You don't want to walk in with your hair mussed, your shirt untucked, and generally looking disheveled. Take a few deep breaths to calm your nerves to gain some brownie points. You don't have anything to lose.

Say, "I am confident and strong. I am a woman/man who thrives on new challenges and works hard to achieve my goals."

Now, go get 'em, tiger!

- Apologize again

When you finally meet the interviewer and extend your hand for a handshake, tell them you are sorry once more for keeping them waiting. Go easy on the apologies; you don't want to appear too desperate.

Know that this second chance is almost impossible, don't waste time by continually drawing attention to being late. Don't lose focus on why you are there: to show them how awesome you are and to get the job of your dreams.

- Send them a thank you note

You should already be planning to send them a thank you note after the interview. It doesn't matter what time you showed up. You need to take this time to apologize for your lateness again, along with your gratitude for taking the time to have the interview even after you showed up late.

Try to stick to just a few lines.

Try this:

"Dear, Hiring Manager,

Thank you so much for taking the time to meet with me today. I just wanted to apologize one more time for being late. It is not the way I ordinarily conduct myself.

I know this was inconvenient for you and I appreciate how you still took time out of your day to meet with me.

Once again, it was a pleasure, and I'm excited about everything I learned about the company and the role today.

Best regards,

(First and last name)

The best advice is not to be late—if at all possible. Get your clothes ready the night before, and anything else you might need, and leave your house 30 minutes earlier than you usually would. Do whatever it takes to make sure you get there ten minutes early.

Cell Phone Etiquette

In this day and age, our cell phones have become an extension of our body. We hardly ever find ourselves without them. In a study performed by Pew Research Center in 2015, they found that 46% of Americans "couldn't live without" their cell phones. Zogby's survey found that 87% of millennials claim that they are never separated from their phones.

Our cell phones hold cameras, parts of our social lives, entertainment, and calendars. However, when you are getting ready to head into a job interview, do the right thing and turn them off.

When it comes to making sure you have good cell phone etiquette during a job interview, there is one basic tip:

Turn off your phone.

This is extremely simple, yet most people forget or fail to do it. If needed, set a reminder on your phone to turn it off right before your interview. You should also make sure that your phone is completely off—don't put it on vibrate. If your phone were to go off, that buzzing noise is not only going to be distracting, but it will also be embarrassing mid-interview. All of those emails, calls, and texts can wait.

You have done all the hard work to get the interview. You have spent time getting things together for the interview. And you have the perfect laid out plan. However, if you go into that interview and the moment you open your mouth to introduce yourself, your phone starts ringing and playing, "If you like Pina Coladas" at a deafening level, it's probably going to be very hard to recover. This is one example of something that you don't want to end up happening during your job interview. This can be avoided by *turning off your phone*.

You should also make sure you turn off your phone early. Ideally, you need to shut your phone off while you are in your car and then leave the phone there. If you take public transport, turn off your phone before you walk into the building. This is a critical time for first impressions. You will probably be greeted by a receptionist when you walk in, so make sure that you focus on putting your best foot forward. Resist the urge of grabbing your phone if you have to wait a few minutes before you get called back into your interview. Many business reception areas have information about the company in their pictures or other written materials. You should have already done your research about the company, but take some time to read the things in the waiting area.

Take some time practicing being without your phone. Most of the behaviors we have when it comes to our cell phones have become subconscious. We automatically reach into our pockets to make sure that our phone is where it is supposed to be, or when somebody else gets a text. If you keep your phone in your briefcase or car, it will prevent you from doing these things. Take a couple of hours and leave your cell phone someplace that you can't easily access it and see how it feels. Go out with some family or friends and shut your phone off and leave it in your bag—just like you will do during the interview. As a bonus, you might remember what it is like to have an uninterrupted conversation.

That notebook and pen that you should have with you will also serve as a place to write down reminders. When the interviewer gives you information about things, you are going to need to write it in your notebook instead of reaching for your phone to type it out. After the interview, you can transfer the information to your cell phone.

Don't start checking your phone. This means you shouldn't sneak out into the hallway or bathroom to check what is going on in "Facebook land". You are currently in a building that is filled with people who could end up being your coworkers. You want to make a great first impression with everybody there. If you are planning on using your cell phone to send out that thank you note after your interview, wait until you get home or are in your car. It is a good idea to take some time to reflect on your interview before the thank you.

Living without your cell phone is hard. We have all become super dependent on technology. It helps us live our lives, and even your prospective employer understands. However, the odds of them going from prospective boss to current boss is greater if your phone doesn't end up going off in the middle of the interview while they are still getting to know you.

What happens if you do forget to turn off your phone, or at the very least, only silence it so that it doesn't make a noise just vibrates? If you ended up not taking any precautions and your phone does start buzzing or ringing while in the interview, the best thing to do is to turn it off quickly and apologize. Don't take the time to check who it was and don't try to create some lame excuse. The best thing to do is silence it, turn it off, and apologize.

Now, for every rule, there is always an exception or two. If the interviewer specifically asks you to use your phone so that they can view your profiles or social media, then this is okay. This could happen if there is a common friend or if social media plays a part in the job's role that you are applying for.

Finally, the only other reason to still have your phone on is if you are waiting for a severe medical or family call. If this is the case, make sure you tell the interviewer beforehand. They will be more accommodating if you are upfront with this information as if you are interrupted by a phone call, it is going to be expected, and they won't judge you for it.

Tests

You should be pretty well prepared for your interview by this point, but there is one thing that we need to talk about before moving onto the interview itself.

You have likely heard some stories, which have reached urban legend status, about how interviewers can be sadistic and force their interviewees to water for two hours before seeing them. While there may be some truth in the years of job interviews that a candidate was forced to wait for a while, you can almost be sure that it wasn't done intentionally.

That being said, having an interviewee wait five to ten more minutes is something that some interviewers will do. This doesn't mean that they do this to watch you squirm for a little while; this is just a way for an interviewer to know how you might react when things don't go as you expected.

They watch to see if you sit their patiently and stay relaxed and calm. Or, do you go up to the receptionist and start asking or demanding for the interviewer to see you immediately. Or do you decide to storm out after having to wait just a few extra minutes? How you react to this situation before you are hired can end up determining how you are going to react to similar problems once you have been hired.

Since you will probably have a bit of wait-time—if you do show up at the suggested five to ten minutes earlier than your scheduled time—bring along a book or magazine to keep you entertained. Make sure that it is something that you wouldn't be embarrassed to be caught reading. Above everything else, make sure that you don't show annoyance. If the receptionist tells you that it is going to be a couple more minutes, simply respond graciously as if nothing has happened, and then keep your focus on your book or magazine.

These few minutes are probably going to be some of the hardest minutes in your life. Up to this point, you have spent your time getting your things together, dressing, eating, and getting to your interview. Now everything has come to a halt. This halt often causes the best of us to fidget. Resist this temptation. Fidgeting is the last thing that you want to be caught doing. You want to come off as confident and show the company and interviewer that you are the type of person who can handle changes and challenges, not the least of which is having to wait for somebody.

Common Mistakes During the Interview

During the hiring process, you have to know what you shouldn't do during a job interview. This is as important as having strong references and a polished resume.

Just like any other interpersonal interactions, job interviews could be very subjective. Experts have found some common interview mistakes that you have to avoid to improve the chances of having a great interview and making a good impression.

Not Knowing About the Company

You need to approach your job interview just like you would a test. It is essential to study the company you are applying to work for so you can talk about your skills and knowledge regarding being a good fit for the business.

To stand out from the crowd, do enough research so you can talk about their recent merger. It shows you are passionate about the company and the role.

Not having the basic knowledge of the role you are applying for or giving them good examples about their past performance makes you look like you have shown up after finding the company on a Google search.

Interviewers like to ask fundamental questions about your interest in the company, your skills, and your background, along with why you think you would be a good fit.

At the bare minimum, read up on the company and have some anecdotes prepared about some projects you have completed successfully.

You also need to know your interviewer. Be prepared with information about the person who will be conducting the interview. You might find that you have a shared interest you will be able to talk about and build rapport from. You might even realize the interviewer has connections to some of your previous employers.

Besides being thoroughly prepared, it might help to calm your nerves. You gain confidence from being competent.

Not Being Yourself

Now is not the time to be humble. Never assume the interviewer is going to remember each detail from your resume about all the sales goals you reached or the awards you won. Women are known to deflect credit about their accomplishments and need to practice talking about their talents and qualifications.

Not Making Eye Contact

Communication is key in an interview. It is crucial to make eye contact when being spoken to and when speaking. Offer them a firm handshake and sit with a correct posture. Even though you might be nervous, try not to let your nervous energy cause you to fidget.

Common Questions and Wrong Answers

People being interviewed should not bring up the salary first—since it puts them in a weak position to negotiate. Bringing it up too soon might give the interviewer the impression that you are only interested in the perks of the job. Save this for after the job has been offered to you.

You need to be prepared to talk about what salary you do expect just in case they bring up the topic.

- Biggest weakness

When your interviewer asks about your biggest weakness, do not offer them a cute answer like, "I work too hard." Instead, this implies that you are not entirely self-aware or aren't taking them seriously, or can't deal with constructive criticism.

Have an honest but thoughtful answer along with an explanation about how you are working to improve your biggest weakness.

Not Asking Questions or Showing Interest

Many interviewers will leave time toward the end to answer questions for you. Usually, they know that you are examining them as well and want to make it a two-sided conversation. This is also a small test. What questions you ask will reveal how you think and the things that are important to you. It will show that you care enough and would like to know more.

It is a good idea to ask questions throughout the interview to keep it an organic, flowing conversation.

Declining to ask questions can be a fatal mistake; it tells them that you aren't interested in the company, or you think you know everything about them already.

Not preparing any questions also shows them that you don't care, haven't done any homework, or aren't curious. If you freeze up and can't think of one, use an old standby like, "What's the culture like here?" or "What does success look like in this role?"

When they wrap up the interview and ask you if you have any questions, you can reply with something like, "I have many questions, and I'm afraid I might run out of time, so I'll just jump right in."

It will show them you have a great interest in the company.

- Not asking about what comes next

At the end of the interview, if they don't give you any information about what comes next in the process, ask. This shows that you are very interested and will keep you informed.

Talking Badly About Previous Employers

Nothing shows you have a bad attitude like criticizing your past or current employer. The person doing the interview is going to wonder if you will talk about them or the company if they do or don't hire you.

Coming Off Desperate, Arrogant, or Unenthusiastic

You never want to come on too strong, brag until you begin sounding arrogant, and dominate the conversation. Some people who are in marketing or sales usually have strong personalities and take over the interview. You want to examine the interviewer, but you can't let them know you are doing it, as you will be seen as an overbearing control freak.

- Talking over others

Don't you love being in a group of people, and one of them talks over everyone else and takes over the conversation? Think about a person who fits this description. Now, would you want to interview this type of person? The odds are you won't.

If you are an excessive talker, you have to know when to share the conversation and when to close your mouth. If you do not, you will ruin your interview without even realizing it. The problem is that most people don't know they fit into this category.

- Talking too much

When you begin rambling, you waste the interviewer's time, and you won't be able to cover everything you want to. Communication skills are excellent to have for many positions, so the interviewer might be trying to see if you can talk with brevity and clarity.

Take the time to listen to the question that they are asking, and give them time to finish their sentence without interrupting them. Never end their sentences for them. When you do talk, notice the balance that you create when talking with them. If you don't, your interview might come to an abrupt close.

- Answers are too long

You might also ruin your interview if you give long answers to simple questions. This is common with any job seeker who has over twenty years of experience. You have much experience, but don't lose your interviewer's interest by telling them every single thing you have ever done.

Many interviewers want to hire candidates who work well in a team. They want a person who interacts well with coworkers and clients. People who talk too much don't fit into this description—since many people look at them as busybodies, forceful, and untrustworthy.

A leading cause of low employee morale and employee turnover goes back to poor management. Leaders have to set examples and show respect for their employees by making an environment where they feel their opinion is valued. Other staff members won't receive well constant talkers—since they tend to have a one-sided view of the way things need to run and have a hard time validating the opinions of others. This can cause workplace friction.

Sales managers are reluctant to hire constant talkers since they don't get favored by most of their clients. Why? They often force their opinions on them, have a hard time listening to others viewpoints, and are too focused on their agendas. They could cause the company to lose clients. If you are applying for a sales position, you have to listen to this advice. You have to demonstrate that you have effective communication skills all through the interview.

- Moments of silence

Don't get restless during silent moments, especially if there is a panel of interviewers. The interviewer/s might be thinking about their next question, taking notes, or thinking about your last reply. During these times, you don't need to continue to talk or start rambling about something irrelevant.

If your natural tendency is to talk a lot or fast, try to speak slower and pause to give others time to talk. You have to practice this a lot even when out with friends or family. Remember: being able to have a good conversation is knowing how to listen and when to talk.

- Showing low energy

This is an interview killer. Here is what it looks like: a lack of enthusiasm, slow to respond to questions, no or little eye contact, and slumped shoulders. If you want the job, showing these signs will make it impossible to persuade anyone to hire you.

- Too Arrogant

It doesn't matter how much experience you have, how attractive you are, or your education level; if you begin acting like you are more important or better than anyone else, most of the time, a company will not hire you.

It is hard to realize you might be arrogant if you cannot humble yourself and take an honest, hard look at your life, workplace environment, personal life, or friendships. If you are thought of as being arrogant or prideful, then the person doing the interview will see you this way too. There isn't anything wrong with being assertive and confident, but being overbearing and egotistical will bring the interview to a close quickly.

Don't confuse confidence and arrogance. A confident leader can discuss their accomplishments and experiences positively without having to belittle other people. They know they can achieve great things. They don't have to force any attention on to themselves since they can inspire others just by being themselves. Surprisingly, by the end of the interview, you might have inspired the interviewer too.

Arrogant leaders will irritate an interviewer. It will be hard for them to talk about their actions. They think their charm and wit will master the interview, but they are very wrong. Trying to be subtle doesn't work for an arrogant person. Interviewers can easily see this character flaw. If a weak area is pointed out, like little to no experience, that has a hard time responding without becoming condescending or exaggerating about accomplishments. Here is a sample:

Interviewer: "I see you have less than two years of experience in leading a global team. We are looking for people who have ten or more years of experience."

Applicant: "I don't think you need to have many years of experience leading a global team to know what you are doing. I have been doing this for less than two years, and my team is now leading in sales as a result of some new systems I implemented. Now all the managers who have been doing this for many years come to me for advice."

You might think there isn't anything wrong with the applicant's answer but look closer. His answer might be correct, but the delivery is entirely wrong. To paraphrase, he has told the interviewer that "you don't need much experience," and that they "don't know what they are talking about since I am number one, everyone asks my advice, and I am the new kid on the block." Here is a better way to answer the question:

Interviewer: "I see that you have less than two years of experience in leading a global team. We are looking for people who have ten or more years of experience."

Applicant: "Yes, that is true, and I have learned a lot during this time. I am very pleased to see that my division is now leading the region in sales in a short time. I highly respect the other seasoned managers who have been doing this for a long time, and I am humbled that they now ask my advice to learn about some systems my team and I have implemented."

Did you see the difference? This second one says the same thing but has a balance of humility and confidence that will make the interviewer like the person more. They are saying the same thing without being arrogant. They also gave respect to other workers who have more years of experience. Instead of them taking complete ownership of the success and new system, they also gave credit to their team.

Here are some responses to stay away from:

1. Brag response

It is fine to sell yourself and convince the interviewer that you are the best person for the job, but you have to avoid exaggerating your accomplishment. Never make an interviewer feel bad when they ask an obvious question.

They might ask if you have any marketing experience, and you respond with laughter and say, "That's all I have done for the past ten years." Understand that all interviewers are professionals; if you make them feel inadequate, the interview is finished.

2. "I" response

If you always start a sentence with "I" instead of "we" or "our", you are doing more harm than good. When you overuse the word "I", it might be interpreted as you "loving to take credit for everything". Start watching out for this if you are interviewing for a job that is part of a team.

3. Professor response

If anyone has ever told you that you respond like you are condescending or lecturing, you have to work on your presentation skills. This happens when people who have big egos give complicated long answers rather than brief replies.

These people get pleasure when they explain complex, intricate details about their jobs. If this sounds like you, try working on your tone, simplify your answers, and ease up on the attitude. Interviewers don't like to feel as if they are listening to a lecture.

- Getting to the interview late

Because candidates for a job usually have interviews with different managers that are scheduled one after the other, two things might happen if you show up late: your first interview might be cut short, or you disrupt other interviewer's schedule. Neither one will be good for you because it will either make many people upset or shorten your interview time.

- Forgetting to follow up

Many people forget the basic rule of interviewing: Follow up within one day by email to thank them for the interview, their time, and to show you are very interested in the role. If you don't, the hiring manager might think you aren't organized or interested. They might just forget about you.

- Arriving too early

Looking at the other side of it, getting to the interview too early can also make the hiring manager mad because it disrupts their schedule. It is a good idea to get there ten minutes early to get through security (if they have it) and check in with the receptionist. It allows you time to use the restroom, prepare for the interview, and compose yourself. It is a gross mistake to get there any earlier than fifteen minutes before your interview.

- Asking personal questions

Some people get so nervous that they forget etiquette and get too personal with their questions. Never ask an interviewer why they left their previous job for their current one, where they have worked, or any details about their family. These questions might make the interviewer feel very uncomfortable and does not show them anything about you.

- Following up aggressively

Yes, it is vital that you follow up, but you shouldn't send multiple emails or call the interviewer. It is very awkward to get a call from somebody who demands to know why they haven't heard back from you. Send them an email and move on with your life. Anything more than one email is way too much.

- Focusing on themselves

If you look at things from the perspective of the employer, the job interview is supposed to help them determine whether or not you will be a good match for the needs of the company. This means your answers need to focus on how the company is going to benefit from your expertise and how you are going to benefit from having the job.

Talking on and on about what you want, how this job is the right direction for your career, and how this experience will be great for you is entirely meaningless to the person doing the interview.

Companies don't hire you to help you; they hire you because you have skills that will help them reach their goals. Your responses will show how you can help the company.

Use a friendly tone but make sure you don't cross the line by sharing too much information. Remember: you don't know how the interviewer will react to being told about your weekend shenanigans. You only get so much time, so you need to remain focused on your accomplishments and the needs of the company.

- Using your cell phone

Even if you are only seeing what time it is, looking at your cell phone might show them you are easily distracted, or rude. Before going into the interview, turn off any devices and put them away. You might be used to taking notes with your phone, but during a job interview, use a notebook.

- Gushing

Never overcompliment the company or the interviewer. You might begin to sound disingenuous.

- Getting angry or desperate

Having these traits is very unattractive to interviewers. It doesn't matter how strongly you might hate your current job or how desperate you are to get a new job; you have to keep your emotions under control during an interview.

Lying to Get the Job

Do you like being lied to? Of course not. And the person interviewing you isn't going to like it either. Saying you are qualified for something when you are not will cause big problems in your future. This never turns out right. When the company finds out the truth, and they will, you will get fired.

Experienced human resource managers are very familiar with deceitful practices like inaccurate accomplishments, incorrect salary, imprecise education, misleading skill sets, wrong job titles, exaggerated employment dates, and false company listings.

So many people throw away wonderful job opportunities because they decided to lie on their resume, during the interview, or on the job application. Many will get away with it, and most HR departments can't investigate every single applicant, but if you continuously do this and don't change, the chances are that one day you will have to confront the truth. It is possible for you not to get the job or lose it after you were hired if you lied during the application process.

Think about how it would feel to get a phone call from your interviewer after they have gotten your background check and they tell you that your employment dates are wrong, and they can't offer you the job because of that.

Another example of lying is rounding off or increasing your hourly wage. If you make $17.30 an hour, don't be tempted to record it as $18 an hour. This goes for employees who are on a salary too. If you earn $53,000 per year and get a bonus of $10,000, don't record your annual base salary as $63,000.

Your best approach is always honesty. Use job skills and experience as your bargaining tools instead of an exaggerated pay scale to adjust income. Also, use your commissions and bonus structure as a way of negotiating a job offer.

Just remember that deceitfulness and lying won't just damage your credibility but can cause you to lose the job. In many cases, like in executive positions, references can't be done until the employee has given their notice to leave their current job. Could you imagine giving your current employer your notice and then realizing that your prospective employer has taken away the job offer? This happens more often than most people realize.

Here is an example of what lying about your skills could do to your future:

A man goes to a job interview and tells his potential employer that he is an expert at programming. To be truthful, his skill set is only in the beginner to intermediate level. He is hired and given the position of programming manager. They offer him a six-figure annual salary. He quits his current job, buys a house, marries his long-time girlfriend, and thinks life is fantastic.

Within one month, he is fired from his position because his employer finds out that he doesn't know much about the specific programming skill he said he was an expert at.

The man thought he could deceive his employer by saying the right words to get through the interview. However, once he had to do the task in front of his boss, he finally admitted that he didn't know how to run the program. Thus, he lost his job.

You have to remember to be honest about what information you give to prospective employers to steer clear of unfortunate and embarrassing circumstances.

Never lie; it is that simple. If you didn't finish that degree because you are missing one class, don't say you have the education requirements. If you don't have a specific skill, don't lie and risk getting exposed. Remain truthful and bring confidence to the interview. Know that you were hired because you represented yourself truthfully and they are getting everything you said you are.

Looking Unpolished

Many people will form an opinion of you in the first seven seconds of meeting you. That doesn't mean you have to wear a designer suit or dress for a job interview for an executive or management position; however, you do need to know some things about the corporate climate and culture of the company before you reach into your closet and grab that perfectly tailored suit or dress.

For some, this won't be a big problem—since you know how to dress for interviews within your industry. But know that all employers and industries aren't the same. What might be acceptable in one environment might be a huge mistake in another.

Dressing too fancy might make you stand out and ruin any chance of getting hired. What do you think would happen if you walked into a machine shop in a tailored suit for an interview. It won't go down too well because most of the people in the place are going to look at you like you are afraid of "getting your hands dirty".

It is imperative to know the culture and climate of a company before you decide how to dress. It is unfortunate that people are so judgmental, but they are. You don't want to get picked on just because of the way you dressed.

Here is an example of dressing too nice:

Early on in a recruiter's career, the recruiter advises a woman, who is about to interview for a management position, to wear a nice dress. The recruiter thinks the woman looks very nice and appropriately attired. Later on that day, the interviewer calls the recruiter and tells them they aren't sure the woman is the right fit for the company. They say their company is very laid back and she was overdressed. Nobody could get past how nice she had dressed. The interviewer also tells the recruiter how their customers are also laid back and prefer a manager who doesn't look like a shiny sales representative.

The recruiter is baffled; they have tons of experience and were confident that the woman was perfect for the job. They can't believe the company is throwing away a perfect candidate just because of the way she was dressed. It makes no sense at all. The recruiter tries every way possible to change the company's mind. They remind them of all the experience the woman has, but nothing will persuade them otherwise. They can't look past the tailored dress, patent leather shoes, designer briefcase, etc. The woman had put her best foot forward but, unfortunately, got rejected because the company could not relate to her. They formed an opinion of her in just seconds, and no amount of experience will change their minds.

Was this example fair? No! However, this is the world we live in. When you are interviewing for jobs, remember that people will hire someone they like and can relate to.

Now, on the other end of the scale, that doesn't mean you should wear jeans and a T-shirt to an interview for a managerial position. However, perhaps tone down your attire to a dress shirt, slacks, and maybe a jacket. That said, let's now talk about dressing too provocatively for an interview.

This is becoming a huge problem that nobody addresses. Interviewers are not going to tell you that your skirt is too short, your blouse is cut too low, or your clothing fits too tightly—not to your face anyway.

Once you leave the interview, you think you blew their minds, but what you don't realize is that the interview was over the moment you stepped into the room. Don't do this to yourself. Dress modestly and let the person conducting the interview focus on you, your resume, and your experience so they can see how great you are.

One more thing: go easy on colognes and perfumes. Yes, they might smell wonderful on you, but strong scents can be distracting. Plus, some people might be allergic to certain smells.

Everyone knows not to judge a book by its cover, but interviewers will. If you show up to an interview looking disheveled or too informal, you will make a bad impression before you even get the chance to introduce yourself.

When you look professional, it shows that you care about the interview and are trying to put your best foot forward. Too many people go to an interview with clothes that are stained, wrinkled, rumpled, and generally, do not fit. You don't have to look like you stepped out of the pages of a magazine, but you need to select your outfit carefully, fix your hair, and take a general look in the mirror before going to your interview.

Forgetting Your Resume

In a perfect world, the interviewer will have your resume ready in hand, but everyone's days are busy, and not everybody can be super organized. This means you always need to have a copy for every person you think you will meet, plus extras in case you get another interview. It is not just helpful but shows you are prepared and thoughtful.

Not Being Available During Business Hours

It might be hard to fit a job interview into your schedule if you are still working a full-time job. However, the interviewer wants to do the interviews during their working hours, so you need to be prepared to take a vacation day if necessary.

Being Rude

You need to try to make a good impression on anyone you meet. You don't know whose opinion will count during the hiring process.

You need to be nice to everybody because many people in management roles will ask the parking attendant, receptionist, and clients if you were respectful to them.

Talking About Illegal Activities

This is not the time to talk about your hobbies or recreational drug use that might violate the employer's conduct policies or laws.

Talking About the Interview On Social Media

Never post anything that you do not want your potential new employer to see. You might also end up tipping your current employer off with regards to how you are looking for a new job.

Bad Interviews

Once you have been asked to come in for an interview, it feels great. And it is. It is the first step to acquiring your dream job. However, to interviewers, it is just another day for them. Interviewers usually conduct hundreds, possibly thousands, of interviews every year. Being unprepared for the interview can be the "kiss of death" for many.

This isn't meant to discourage you or suggest that the people conducting the interview don't care. The main point is that they go through this process a lot more than you do. When you give them what you think is an exciting, unique, or thought-out response, they might have heard it many times in just one week. If you want to stand out, you have to avoid clichéd answers and dig deep into the information they are looking for.

There are many ways you can blow an interview. The worst answers can show the interviewer flaws with your preparation, attitude, and interest in the job qualifications to get the job done. They could also show you can't work well with others or you have a bad work ethic.

What responses are the worst offenders? Some of the answers are scary, and some are funny. It would be much better to get prepared and stay away from giving any of these answers during your job interview. We talked with many career coaches, HR professionals, recruiters, and other experts to get their opinion.

These answers to typical job interview questions show either a total lack of being prepared or no understanding of how to have a successful interview. Regardless, the results will always be the same: a lost opportunity. These are some answers to stay away from no matter what:

Q: Tell me about yourself?

A: Details about your professional flaws, medical history, or details about your family life.

"There isn't much to tell."

"I'm a rock musician. I'm a drummer. Our agent quit, and we don't have any gigs for the rest of the year. We are looking for a new agent, and I hope to get back to that soon. That is what I do."

"I am a huge Yankees fan, avid softball player, and I have the gift of gab. I'm usually the life of every party."

Q: What are your greatest strengths?

A: "I'm a team player."

"I don't know, but I am a good learner."

"I do good work."

"I'm the best."

Q: What do you know about the company?

A: Avoiding giving them a straight answer.

"I heard you pay well."

"You have a job opening."

Visible details like their industry.

Q: Why should we hire you?

A: "It sounded like a fun job."

"I am the best person for the job."

"I am a hard worker."

"I am great with people."

"I need a job."

"I need money."

"Nobody else will hire me."

"I'm desperate."

"I'm unemployed."

"I don't know."

Q: What are your most significant weaknesses?

A: "I'm not good with the newest version of Microsoft Office."

"I can't do spreadsheets."

"I don't like dealing with difficult people."

"I don't have any."

"I have a lot; it is hard to choose just one."

"I don't spell well."

"I'm a perfectionist."

"I work too hard."

"I can't think of any."

"I have been known to lose my patience with incompetent people."

Q: Tell me about your last job?

A: "You have my resume right there; didn't you read it?"

Q: Why do you want to work here?

A: "I need a job."

"My mom said I had to get a job."

"I hear you give great employee discounts."

"I look great in a uniform."

"I can walk to work from where I live."

Q: Why are you the right candidate for this position?

A: "I'm passionate about it."

Q: Where do you see yourself in five years?

A: "Still doing this job."

"Doing your job."

"I hate this question."

Q: What is your greatest strength?

A: "I'm a team player."

Q: Do you have any questions for me?

A: "How much is the employee discount?"

"How much vacation time do I get?"

"I don't have any questions."

"Do I have to work overtime?"

"No."

"Would you like to go out for a drink?"

"Is there a limit on how much I can buy?"

"Can I resell?"

"Do I get paid sick days? How many do I get every month?"

"How often do we get raises?"

"Do you conduct background checks?"

"Do you check references?"

"Do I have to pass a drug test before I get hired? How much notice do you give before the test?"

Q: Do you work well with others?

A: "I work fine with most people, but others bother me a lot."

"My coworkers don't like me, but I think it's because I intimidate them."

Q: Why did you apply for this position?

A: "I saw it in the jobs listings, and it seemed interesting."

Q: Why did you get fired?

A: "I missed too many days."

"I failed a drug test."

Q: What did you like least about your previous position?

A: "I hated the job and the company. They were awful to work for."

Good Interviews

You might be wondering what steps you can take to have a great job interview. Well, you have chosen the right book. This chapter will guide you through the whole process from getting yourself prepared, the day of the interview, what questions might be asked, and the waiting game after the interview.

Here is a secret that might help you relax a bit: the people conducting the interview actually want you to do well. It is not easy for them to find the perfect person for the job. You will make their day better if you wind up being the person they are looking for.

So, to prepare yourself, instead of looking at the interviewer as somebody who is trying to "mess you up", it will help if you thought about them as a person who is cheering you on. That doesn't mean some of them won't try and trip you up, but with the tips below, you will be ready for them.

Getting Ready for the Interview

What should you do to have a great job interview? Here are some tips that will help.

Remember that success begins before you even walk in the door.

1. Review the job description carefully

Look up everything that you don't understand. This helps you to make sure you answer all of their needs.

2. Make notes

Write down some notes using the job description and resume. Think about some stories that are related to the job you are applying for or from somewhere else if you think it will help you get your point across.

You can use these to show the interviewer how you have gone above and beyond to solve an issue, made a new method, overcome weaknesses, helped during a critical situation, or helped to reach a successful outcome. You might not have to use every story you know, but it is smart to have some just in case you need them.

3. Research the company

If you didn't look the company up before you applied for the job, you need to do so now. There isn't anything less impressive than chatting with someone without knowing anything about the company. If at all possible, look for information about the person who will be interviewing you. Use this information sparingly, or it might seem like you are stalking them. Use GlassDoor.com or LinkedIn to help with research. They can give you some great insights.

4. Practice

Answer the most popular interview questions that you will find later in this chapter to help you. Do this in front of a mirror or have a friend do some mock interviews with you.

You need to be comfortable talking about yourself and all the things you have accomplished that you can bring to the company. Try not to sound like you are bragging or are too self-conscious. Be yourself and remember you are only having a conversation with another person.

5. Know your resume

You would be amazed at the number of people who have stuttered when asked about the experience they have listed on their resume. It is surprising to interview someone who can't remember what they have listed on their resume or when they learned a specific skill.

Interview Day

1. Turn off your cell phone

This is easy to forget, but it isn't necessarily a deal breaker. It might be for some, but it is annoying. Try to remember to turn it off or leave it in your car or purse.

2. Dress professionally

Match your look to what you know about the company and what they require. Look them up online or go by the company to see how their employees dress. If they allow casual dress like T-shirts and jeans, don't wear this to the interview though. Wear a pair of nice slacks or a skirt along with a dress shirt and jacket. A suit would be too formal.

Don't be too much: haute couture (even if this is the type of job, don't try to wow them), avant-garde, casual, elegant, or sexy (cover up the assets). Less is always more here.

3. Resume

Always bring extra copies of your resume. Professionals do misplace things.

4. Feeling nervous

If you begin to feel super nervous before you leave for your interview, try doing some exercise. You don't want to go all out and get super sweaty, especially if you know you won't have time to shower. Singing or some simple jumping jacks can help get rid of the jitters. Nerves are very normal and okay since nerves can be channeled into other energy.

Meditation or yoga can help too. Believing in yourself and being prepared is the best medicine.

5. While you are waiting

While you are sitting in the waiting area don't prop your feet up on chairs or tables, slurp your coffee, slump, put on makeup, hum, scroll through your tablet or phone, chew gum, or—seriously—have parents or children with you. It's amazing how often this happens.

You have to be prepared to wait patiently, no matter for how long. Look as energized and pleasant as possible. Use this time to think about your stories and how your experience will fit in with the company. Observe everything you can during this time because you are trying to decide if you want to work here too.

6. The receptionist is a great ally

At least they shouldn't try to sabotage you. You might be wondering how this is important, but it is reminding you of one important fact: what comes out of your mouth is just one part of the interview process; first impressions are a huge part of the interview.

The interview isn't going to begin when the person doing the interview walks into the room and shakes your hand. It also doesn't end when you walk out of their office. Anybody at any step of this process can share information about you. Be nice to everyone.

7. Remain positive

No matter the context, always remain levelheaded and positive throughout the interview process. Getting angry or annoyed by small or trivial things, such as the interviewer not smiling at you, won't do you any favors. Instead, it will kill your chances of getting the job.

What Not To Say

1. Look the interviewer in the eye

When the interviewer walks into the room, look them in the eye, smile, and shake their hand. When shaking hands, don't go for the death grip, just a nice firm shake. Say something nice.

2. Never lie

Don't ever lie, even if you have to admit you don't know something. If it is applicable, show interest in learning about new things. You could tell the interviewer that you have started looking into it and add your question about what they just asked. This shows you are truly interested. A good employer doesn't expect you to know everything.

3. Never use canned answers

When you are in an interview, trust that you have done everything possible up to that moment. Answer in YOUR words and make sure you heard correctly what they asked. People looking for a job will overprepare themselves to the point that they put a canned answer to a question that wasn't asked.

This is never a good idea. It tells the interviewer you aren't listening. Turn to your stories, but be conversational. Too many memorized words will lose the human connection you are trying to build.

4. Never say you don't have questions for them

Don't ever tell them that you don't have any questions for them. Prepare some questions in advance. Feel free to take some notes and use things you have learned during the interview to find a question. This earns big points.

For the final question, if you feel things have gone well, let them know how interested you are and ask when they might get back in touch with you.

5. Stay away from jokes

Jokes can fall flat at times. Humor is fine if it feels right and if the interviewer is funny. Feel free to laugh at their jokes. Never, ever, fake laugh. They will see right through it. Do a small chuckle or smile.

Winning an interview

1. Look them in the eye

When you walk into the interview, shake the interviewer's hand and smile. Never shake hands like you are trying to rip their hand off. Just something firm and friendly.

2. Use real-life stories

You have researched the company. You have read the job description. Make sure you can match your experience and stories to what the company is looking for. Tell them how you have solved problems.

3. Practice

Before the day of your interview, go through standard interview questions with someone you trust.

4. More than one interviewer

If there is more than one person in the room while you are being interviewed, direct the answer to the person who asked the question. Be sure to make eye contact with every person at some point.

5. Speak clearly

Speak at a normal conversational pace. Remember to breathe.

6. Keep eye contact

Maintain eye contact, keep the energy up, and listen. If you realize you are beginning to think ahead about how to answer, or what they might ask later, stop yourself. You are going to lose more than you gain by jumping ahead. Trust yourself and stay in the moment. Make a connection and show them that you will be an asset to their team.

7. Still nervous?

If you are still feeling a bit nervous, it is fine to mention you are nervous if you think it might help get rid of some of the discomfort. The interviewer expects nerves. Add in some words about how excited you are for the opportunity. Stay brief and move on and answer their questions.

8. When the interview is over

Remember to smile and shake hands once the interview is over. Shake hands with everyone in the room and thank each person.

After the Interview

1. Thank you note

Some people say this isn't important. It might not be in many cases, and it probably isn't going to change your chances. If you send one, though, make it short and pleasant. It will leave a great impression. Snail mail is excellent, but email is fine too.

2. Follow up

After the interview is over, the time you wait to hear if you've been successful will test the patience of the most confident and most energetic person. It might take a day, or even months to hear back from them, even if you were their top candidate. Even in the best of circumstances, it might go beyond what they told you it would, especially if more than one person is making the decisions.

This is when you need to continue to look and find things to keep yourself occupied. Once a couple of weeks have passed, and you still haven't heard from them, it is fine to call and inquire about your status. Let them know you are still interested. You could also ask if there is anything else you can give them to make their decision easier.

They usually never forget. Even if you didn't follow up or send them a thank you, if you are the best candidate, they will contact you.

How to Improve Your Interview Skills

The best way to improve your skills is to do practice interviews. Ask a friend to pretend they are interviewing you. Don't allow them to take it easy on you either. Run it like a real interview. Record yourself so you can watch it later.

Most Common Questions

How many questions your interviewer asks could be limitless. The following is a list of the most commonly asked questions and how you can answer them in ways that will make you more memorable. Even the standard questions can have smart answers.

Take the time to read through all of these questions and think about them carefully. Think about how you would answer them if asked. Being prepared is the key to success. Not being prepared is a grave mistake; it shows the potential employer that you don't have any interest. Prepare your answers to these common questions:

- Tell me about yourself

This isn't a question but an invitation to share things about yourself that you think are important. Talk about why you worked at specific jobs. Say why you left them. Explain why you went to a certain school and grad school. What were your reasons behind it? Explain why you backpacked through Europe for one year and what you learned from the experience. While answering the questions, connect the dots on your resume so the interviewer can understand not only what you have done but why you did it. This is your chance to show how you are different from the other candidates.

- What are your weaknesses?

Everyone knows the way to answer this: choose weakness and magically change it into a strength.

Here is an example of an answer: "My biggest weakness is being too absorbed in my work that I lose all track of time. Each day I look up and realize everybody else has gone home. I know I should be more aware of the clock, but when I love what I'm doing, I can't think about anything else."

This means that your biggest weakness is that you put in more hours than everybody else. That's great; however, a better way to approach this is to choose an actual weakness that you are trying to improve and tell the interviewer what you have been doing to overcome it. Nobody is perfect, but if you can show them that you are honestly willing to look at yourself and find ways to improve, you will get pretty close.

- Where do you see yourself in five years?

Your interviewer doesn't care that you want to be a supervisor and climb the corporate ladder. If you aren't interviewing for a supervisory position, they don't care about your management skills. You can tell them how you have mentored others and led projects without supervision. That shows them you have leadership skills.

You could tell them something like how in five years you could make a huge impact on the company's future. Think about ways you can do this in the position that you are interviewing for. If you are interviewing for a career in technology, you need to advance your skills here too. You also need to share the areas you need to strengthen. Make sure these areas of expertise are what the company is needing.

- What are your strengths?

Not sure why interviewers insist on asking this question since they are looking at your resume and it shows your strengths. However, if you are asked this question, give them an on point, sharp answer. Be precise and clear. If you are great at solving problems, don't tell them that; instead, give them some examples that can prove you are great at solving problems. If you are an intelligent, emotional leader, also don't tell them that; instead, give them some examples that show you know how to answer their unasked questions.

Don't claim to have specific attributes; you have to prove the attributes to them.

- Why should we hire you?

This is a differentiation question. They want you to tell them that they would be crazy not to hire you.

Let them know that you possess almost all the experience they are looking for and you have a few extra abilities that they don't know they need as of yet. Make them understand that you are a person who will not only meet their needs but will be a valuable asset for the future.

Will they need a different set of skills as the company grows?

You might have skills that you saw in a different job description they want to fill.

You can mention this, and they might let you help with some of those jobs until they find somebody to hire for that position or you could be the new hire's backup.

Have you done some things that they are just now beginning? Having these "skills" to offer is a great plus for any job candidate.

- How do others describe you?

Here is another opportunity to diversify yourself. Everybody says they are a team player, good communicator, and a hard worker.

How many are leaders in their industry, game changers, and problem solvers?

Get creative and have stories to tell. Your interviewer wants to know why somebody thinks you are any of the above.

You want to give them attributes that show them you are the go-to person no matter where you work. Even normal answers can be tweaked to make you more valuable:

1. Yes, they want people who will work hard, but that is normal for any workplace. You might work hard, but you help others work smarter, not harder. You help them do their jobs better, and this makes their jobs much easier.

2. Anybody can communicate well. This doesn't just mean speaking well; this also includes listening. Are you always hearing things that other people don't? Can you understand how to do things fast? Do you understand what people are trying to tell you with body language and other clues?

3. Every job expects you to be a team player. What does being a team player mean? Does it mean you have to get along with everybody? This isn't hard to do if you are nice. What about pulling your weight? This is again expected. What have you accomplished that goes beyond your job description that helped the team meet that impossible deadline, and what did you do that saved your team from disaster?

- How did you hear about the job opening?

Job fairs, online listings, general postings, job boards—most people find their job this way, so it isn't a wrong answer. A person who continually finds each job from general postings just hasn't figured out what they want to do. They are only looking for any job they can find.

Don't explain how you heard about the job; *show* them you heard about it because you either follow the company, heard about it from one of their current employees, or through a colleague. Show them you knew about the job because you wanted to work there.

Companies don't want to hire someone who only wants a job; they want to hire somebody who wants to work at their company.

- When can you start?

You have to be careful about how you answer this question for many reasons:

This doesn't mean you have the job. They might want to know to put it in their notes. You have to keep your guard up until you have finished the interview and are driving away.

If you are still employed at another company, you need to be honest about the start date and show some professionalism. You need to tell them you have to talk with your current company and see if they require specific notice before leaving the job. If you have a crucial role in the company, your new employer will expect a transition period too.

If you can begin right away, by all means, tell them tomorrow. Having a sense of urgency and excitement about beginning work for a new company is a great thing.

- Why do you want this particular job?

This answer should be a heartfelt one, and your gut will give you the answer. If your answer has to do with benefits, work schedule, location, money, or other factors that don't have anything to do with the job, you might want to think a bit more. These reasons are not relevant to the interviewer.

You need to dig deep on this answer. Don't just talk about why the company will be a great one to work for. Talk to them about how the position will be a perfect fit for what you want to accomplish both long and short term.

They want to hear that this is your dream job. This job is your next step toward your desired career.

Be ready for their follow up question: How so?

You need to answer this honestly and tell them exactly how this job meets your professional needs and how you can contribute to your highest ability while at the company. People like to feel as if their work means something. There isn't anything wrong with sharing your feelings thoughtfully.

If you can't figure out why the position will be a perfect fit, you need to look elsewhere. Life is too short.

- Tell me about your dream job?

There are three words that you need to use to answer this question: relevance, relevance, relevance.

This doesn't mean you have to make up an answer. You should be able to learn something from each job you have. Try to work backward; find things about the position that will help you if you were to find your dream job one day. Tell them how these things are relevant to what you want to do someday.

Don't worry about admitting that you may someday move on, whether to join a different company or begin your own business. Employers don't expect anybody to work for them forever.

- Why are you leaving your current job?

This question could be a deal breaker.

Let's begin with things you shouldn't say. NEVER talk about how difficult your boss is. NEVER talk about not getting along with others. NEVER talk bad about the company. NEVER mention that your role or compensation is below your standards.

There might be legitimate reasons for leaving a job:

1. The current employer might not be able to give you any professional growth.

2. The current employer or department might be unstable.

Find a reason that the interviewer can't be worried about.

Try to focus on all the positive things a change of employers would bring. Tell them about what you would like to achieve. Tell them what you want to learn. Tell them about how you want to grow and the things you want to accomplish. Tell them how a move will be great for you and the company.

If you have a problem that concerns you that might be a deal breaker, by all means, mention it. Be prepared for them to take it one way or another. You might only want to work for a company that buys from vendors within a specific company. The interviewer will tell you if their company does this. If not, the interview will probably be over.

When you complain about your current employer, you are entertaining gossip. If you speak badly about one employer, you will do it with another.

- What work environment works best for you?

You might like working alone, but if you are interviewing for a job in a call center, using this answer is bad.

Take some time and think about the job you are interviewing for along with the culture of the company. If you like a flexible schedule, but the company doesn't have one, focus on another place. If you like to have support and direction, but the company wants its employees to be able to self manage, find another place.

Try to find ways the company will work for you. If you cannot find these, don't take the job. You will be miserable every single day.

- Why did you leave your last job?

This one is a bit tough. You shouldn't quit one job until you have another. However, life doesn't always work out this way. Did you leave because you didn't have enough time to look for your next job? Or because the company you were working for was closing, and you decided not to waste time waiting for them to shut the doors?

Many reasons are considered a necessity:

1. Harsh working conditions

2. Had to move to a new location for whatever reason

3. Health or family reasons

The only way to answer this question is to keep the answer short. Never try to expand your answer or include details.

- What was the hardest decision you've had to make in the past six months?

This question's goal is to see how well the person's reasoning ability, willingness to take risks, judgment, and problem-solving skills are.

Not having an answer would be a warning sign for a potential employer. Everybody makes hard decisions, no matter their position.

A good answer would prove that you can make hard reasoning based on an analytical decision. For example, would you be willing to wade through reams of data to figure out the best solution for the problem?

A great answer would prove you can make hard interpersonal decisions or hard data-driven decisions that might include interpersonal ramifications and considerations. Being able to make decisions that are based on data is helpful since almost all decisions will have an impact on most people. The best candidates will weigh up all sides of a problem, not just the human or business side.

- Why did you get fired?

This is a dangerous zone. This isn't the time to defend yourself with a sob story about being a victim.

If you made a mistake, you have to minimize how severe the situation was. Some might describe arguing with a boss as a difference of opinion. If your moral compass told you not to follow orders, this could be considered as "taking the high road".

NEVER cast the blame on other people. Think about finding a silver lining. Did you learn from the experience and thus now have some knowledge that will lessen the chances of it ever happening again?

Being laid off is not the same as being fired. If you were part of a huge company lay off, this is entirely different from being fired. It was a financial decision made by management, as you were in the group that was part of the budget cuts. Layoffs aren't usually personal; they are just business. People who hire staff know this, and have been involved in one at some point in their lives.

- Do you have a leadership style?

This is a rather hard question to answer without using a bunch of old clichés. Try to share leadership examples like, "The best way for me to answer that is to give you some examples of leadership challenges that I have faced," then share some situations where you handle the problem, worked through a crisis or motivated a team. Tell them what you did, and this will give the hiring manager a sense of how you will lead. It also lets you highlight some of your successes.

- Can you explain this gap in employment?

The main thing you need to do here is to make sure you give them a picture of you consistently doing something constructive, helping family, improving yourself, or being productive.

Interviewers don't want to hear that you needed a break from the rat race or you needed to recharge. The first thing that will pop into their minds is: When will you need another break? Will it be in the middle of that big project we have coming up?

- Have you ever disagreed with a manager's decision? How did you handle it?

Nobody will agree with all the decisions. Having disagreements is fine; it's what you do about the conflict that matters. We all know someone who loves to have a meeting after the meeting where they have supported a decision but then try to undermine it after the decision was made.

Show the interviewer you are a professional. Show them you voiced your concerns productively. If you can give them an example that will prove you can create change, wonderful. If not, show them that you support decisions even if you think they are wrong, as long as it isn't immoral or unethical.

Each company wants its employees to be forthright and honest, to share their concerns and issues, but to get behind decisions and support the company just like they agreed, even though they didn't.

- How would others describe you?

This is an awful question, but some interviewers might ask it. Here is a good answer: "I think people would say that what you see is what you get. If I say I am going to do something, I will do it. If I tell you I am going to help, I'll help. I'm not sure that everybody likes me, but they all know they can count on what I say and how hard I work."

- What was your salary in your last job?

This is another hard one. You need to be honest and open, but some companies will ask this question to begin salary negotiations.

Use an approach that skirts around the real issue but still gives them an answer. When they ask, reply with, "I'm focusing on jobs in the $50K range. Does this position pay in that range?" You should already know this, but it is a great way to deflect the question.

The interviewer might ask or they might not. If they press you for a definite answer, you will need to decide for yourself whether or not you want to share. Your answer isn't going to matter all that much since you will either accept the offered salary or not. It all depends on what you think is fair.

- What will we see you do in your first three months with us?

This answer should come from the employer. They should have expectations and plans laid out for you.

If you are asked, you can use the following as a guideline:

1. You will make a difference in bringing teamwork, a sense of commitment, focus, and enthusiasm to other employees and customers.

2. You will work hard to figure out how your job makes value. You won't just keep busy; you will keep busy doing the correct things.

3. You will stay focused on doing the things you do best. You will be hired since you bring specific skills and use these skills to make things happen.

4. You will learn how to help everyone around you: vendors, suppliers, customers, peers, employees, and the boss.

Now all you have to do is put in all the specifics that apply to the job and you.

- There is a snail inside a 30-foot well. Every day he can climb three feet, but each night he slides back down two. How long is it going to take him to get out of the well?

This type of question has become popular thanks to Google. The person doing the interview isn't looking for the correct answer so much as seeing how well you can reason.

The best thing to do if you aren't a math genius is to talk through the problem out loud while you are trying to solve the problem. Never be afraid to laugh at yourself if you get it wrong. At times they are trying to assess how well you deal with failure.

- What do you do when you aren't at work?

Most companies feel that a cultural fit is essential for their company. They take their employees outside interests as a way to figure out if you will fit well with the team they have already established.

Never let yourself be tempted into lying and telling them you like doing things you don't. Focus on hobbies or activities that show growth, such as goals you are working toward or skills you are learning. Put these into your details. Here is an example: "I am raising a family, so most of my time is focused on them, but I am using my commute time to learn Spanish."

- Do you have any questions for me?

You need to have questions. This is your time to interview the interviewer. This is your time to learn more about the company, its leadership style, its corporate culture, its role, and many other things you can think of.

People who are truly interested in the company will ask these questions. People who don't ask questions show they aren't truly interested but just trying to put feelers out to see how it "feels".

You need to know that the interview isn't over just because the interviewer asked this question. Good candidates use this as a time to shine.

You need to ask questions that do these things:

1. Show you have done your research about the company.

2. That will prompt a discussion or have interesting answers.

3. Mentions something else that is interesting and related to you.

Closing the Interview

You might not have a chance to address any shortcomings in an interview to follow up. You have to understand what was missing from the interview while you are still in the middle of the interview.

Once you have asked your questions, you want to confirm that you are the perfect candidate for the job. For you to do this, you have to probe the interviewer's mind and see if they still have concerns about you.

One final question to ask your interviewer is: "After discussing this job, I feel as if I would be a perfect fit for it. I'm curious to know if there is anything I said or DID NOT say that would make you believe otherwise."

Whatever answer you get to this question might open the door to something you weren't able to talk about during the interview or to clarify any misconceptions about something that was said.

Job Interview Checklist

The best way to make sure that you are confident in your interview is to be prepared. This will ensure that you make an amazing first impression and will help ease your nerves. The next time you have an interview, check off each of the following steps as you prepare. You do not have to do these things in the order that they are listed:

- *Get your clothes ready*

  o As you know, how you dress for an interview tells your potential employer a lot. The right outfit will let them know that you understand the company and its environment. This shows that you respect them.

- *Study the job listing*

  o Read back through the job advertisement and description to figure out exactly what the employer is looking for. Then, create a list of your personal and professional qualities, skills, and knowledge that fit into what they want. Make sure that you are ready to describe your attributes that show them you are the perfect fit.

- *Research the company*

  o This should fit right into the last step. Learn as much as you can about the company. This will also help you learn how you should dress for the interview as well. Look over their website, social media, and LinkedIn profiles of past and present employees. If you can, speak will some people who have worked for them. It also helps to get Google News to see if there has been any negative or positive press for them recently.

- *Contact company contacts*

  o To help boost your chances of getting hired, get a referral from a connection within the company. Having contacts who work for the company, or have worked for the company and left on good terms, can provide you with an inside track to getting hired. Potential employers like to interview people who come recommended. The contact can also let you know more about how the company's hiring process works.

- *Look over your resume*

  o If you have been asked for an interview, then they like what they saw on your resume. They are going to ask you about certain things on it, so make sure you are familiar with what it says. If you have a phone interview, you can have the resume in front of you, but you still shouldn't read directly off of it.

- *Come up with accomplishments that you can talk about*

    o Hiring managers love to hear these things. These things should be on your resume, but either way, make sure that you have some facts and stories that you can share during the interview.

- *Find out who the interviewer is*

    o If at all possible, research some of the people that you will have to speak with. This will help you know how to prepare and say the right things to impress them.

- *Practice your interview questions*

    o Take some time to review some of the most common interview questions. This will give you a chance to frame your questions before you get surprised by them in the interview. This will help to reduce your stress. Get a family member or friend involved.

- *Be ready for questions about previous job changes*

    o The interviewer is likely going to ask you why you left your last job or why there is a gap in your employment. Make sure that you are ready to answer these questions. These things aren't bad, but what is bad is if you can't explain why.

- *Practice your technique*

    o What you say and how you act during an interview is either going to help or hinder you. While practicing your answers, practice how you sit, use your hands, and your eye contact.

- *Work on your etiquette*

o Is bringing a cup of coffee or your cell phone okay? How should the interviewer be greeted? What do you need to bring with you? Make sure you brush up on the best interview etiquette so that you don't end up getting caught off guard.

- *Arrange transportation and get directions*

    o You have to know where you're supposed to go for your interview. Make sure you know exactly where to go and how long it will take you so that you aren't late or flustered. Check out the parking situation or public transport. You can also try a test run the day before to make sure that your directions are correct.

- *Have the right things with you*

    o You need to make sure that you know what to bring with you. You may need extra copies of your resume, reference list, a portfolio, and questions that you may have for them. Make sure you have everything ready to go. Pack them up the night before so that you don't forget them.

- *Send a quick thank you*

    o After you have had your interview, take the time to send the interviewer a thank you note. This helps to reinforce the fact that you are interested in the job. This is also a great time to address any concerns or issues that may have come up during the interview.

Conclusion

Thank for making it through to the end of *Job Interview: Will These Mistakes Cost You The Job?* It should have been informative and provided you with all of the tools you need to achieve your goals, whatever they may be.

Yes, job interviews are crazy and stressful, but with the right prep work, you can prove that you are worth a company's time and money. The next time you have an interview lined up, go through the checklist to make sure that you are prepared. The interview is the one thing standing between you and the job of your dreams, so don't let little mistakes prevent you from pursuing your dreams. Follow everything you have learned, and get any job that you want.

Finally, if you found this book useful in any way, a review on Amazon is always appreciated!